Malcolm
McLaren

Malcolm McLaren

The Sex Pistols, the anarchy, the art, the genius – the whole amazing legacy

Ian Macleay

JOHN BLAKE

Published by John Blake Publishing Ltd,
3 Bramber Court, 2 Bramber Road,
London W14 9PB, England

www.johnblakepublishing.co.uk

First published in paperback in 2010

ISBN: 978 1 84358 2786

British Library Cataloguing-in-Publication Data:

A catalogue record for this book is available from the British Library.

Design by www.envydesign.co.uk

Printed in Great Britain by Bookmarque Ltd, Croydon CR0 4TD

1 3 5 7 9 10 8 6 4 2

Papers used by John Blake Publishing are natural, recyclable products made
from wood grown in sustainable forests. The manufacturing processes
conform to the environmental regulations of the country of origin.

For Elizabella Macleay-Wood – isn't she lovely?

ACKNOWLEDGEMENTS

To my wife Marie, who helped so much. To John Blake who I owe so much to. His brilliant team, Rosie Virgo and Joanna Kennedy. My good friend Julian Rigby who contributed greatly and Lynda Hart always a supporter of my ventures. My old amigo Patrick Hagglund gave us some great help with the Grundy stuff. I met Christakis at Malcolm's funeral and his insights gave me a wonderful perspective of the great man. My sister-in-law Fran helped me with the Elvis data.

And to anybody who ever wondered who killed Bambi.

Ian Macleay
July 2010

CONTENTS

THE BOAT TRIP

'If you have enough neck, you can get away with anything.'
MALCOLM MCLAREN

*'As far as I am concerned the Sex Pistols
were an idea, not a band.'*
MALCOLM MCLAREN

The boat was called the *Queen Elizabeth*, funnily enough.

It had a delicious sense of irony about it; all it needed was a Jolly Roger flag with the skull and crossbones. The plan was simple: hire a boat, load it up with the group and an assortment of hangers-on, record-company people and friends, and sail up London's River Thames. Then park up outside the Houses of Parliament, play a few songs and be as obnoxious as possible.

It would be the final insult, playing in their backyard. Theatre of Provocation and all that.

The time was June 1977, the week of the Queen's Silver Jubilee. Bunting everywhere, street parties and bonfires. Malcolm McLaren was 31 years old and the controversial manager of the most notorious rock band of the day – actually, make that *any* day – the Sex Pistols. The group were soon to dominate the charts with their self-penned song 'God Save The Queen', which in one day alone had shifted 150,000 copies. He had hurled a beaker full of urine into the face of the establishment that was to have a seismic effect on the world, changing it musically and culturally. Also, it was to be the last time that music had the power to alter things, to worry people, to make them think.

For McLaren, the moment would never be sweeter. Due to his manipulation, he had caused a tremendous furore about the record before it had even been released, and his tactics provided the group with an attitude suited to the decline in the country. Finally, after being dumped by two companies, he had signed with a third – Virgin – founded by the future billionaire Richard Branson. Whether or not he had any long-term future with the company was open to conjecture. He found it all a bit cosy and relaxed. No tension, no edge. That is what bands thrive on. Once you lost it, you were just another robot, playing the safe ball, being part of the system. Never trust a hippie.

There was to be a Royal flotilla that would go down the Thames against a backdrop of a huge firework display. McLaren thought it would be nice for the Pistols to have their own cruise ship, so, when the boat left Charing Cross pier about 6.30pm, there must have been about 200 people on it. Branson had paid £500 for the privilege of hiring the craft, and a huge banner in the traditional Pistols day-glo yellow and pink colours was draped down one side of it. 'God Save The Queen' – The new single by the Sex Pistols. They thought they would keep it low key.

Soon the music was blaring, a bit of dub; someone put on The Ramones. The bar was packed; they would not serve doubles though. Firewater to the Indians.

The boys started playing on the deck in the covered area. It was very small and there was a problem with the feedback. Who cares though? Starting off with that old favourite 'Anarchy In The UK', perhaps they were the Bay City Rollers of outrage. McLaren watched as Rotten lurched around on the deck. Frustration at not being able to play had gnawed away at him for weeks. Rotten put the same effort into it no matter where he was. Just like that first day in the shop when he swaggered in, such pent-up anger, a model of bravado. 'How can I use this?' McLaren had asked himself. He was still asking that night.

It was a lovely early-summer evening, but got a bit chilly later on. That summer was special but no one spoke about global warming. As the boat neared

Westminster, the party became more raucous; some of the voyagers were really hitting it hard. McLaren gazed down the dirty old river and that is when he spotted the launches packed with police. At first they started 'buzzing' the vessel. Then they clambered aboard like a Royal Navy boarding party storming the *Black Pearl*.

Westwood was always on about pirates, she had been designing some dresses with a piratical theme. Maybe it would catch on, maybe one day you could have a pop singer with that image. Plundering, taking what he wanted.

The police made a beeline for McLaren. They must have been briefed, him and Rotten, the leaders of the gang. Appropriately, they cut the power as John started singing 'No Fun', then they closed the bar and escorted the punks back. They started pushing and shoving, then out came the cuffs. McLaren started to protest, then he swore at them, which is what they charged him with in the morning.

When the punk party disembarked, the press were there already on the jetty, and a lot more police. Like at the football: Paul Cook was always on about the rucks he used to see when he followed Chelsea. The flash bulbs started popping. It's all on YouTube somewhere, and someone later published a book with a lot of pictures taken that night. One iconic image was of McLaren being manhandled by the police: 'Sex Pistols manager led away in handcuffs'. It occurred to him around then that they were in the eye of the maelstrom. The jihad of terror was just starting.

Years later some journo wrote it up like it was some masochistic thrill for McLaren, finally being punished by a father figure. Yeah, sure.

CHAPTER ONE

ROSE CORRE ISAACS

'My grandmother used me to take out her dysfunctional upbringing on the world. She used to say, "You know, McLaren, it's very difficult to be bad. You've got to work at it. But then again... who wants to be good?"'
MALCOLM MCLAREN

Malcolm Robert Andrew McLaren was born the year after the war, on 22 January 1946, the same month as Pink Floyd's Syd Barrett, although it was another Sidney who would play a huge part in his life some years later. George Best was also born later that year, and Frank Capra's *It's A Wonderful Life* was showing at the local cinema. The childhood of Malcolm McLaren, however, was far from wonderful.

McLaren's father Peter, a Scottish engineer, had married Jewish-born Emily Isaacs. The couple had another son, Stewart. 'War babies' was the term given to them; Tom Robinson made a record called after them, used in the soundtrack for TV show *Ashes To Ashes*. Not that Peter had been off to war, far from it. The dominant figure in McLaren's life, however, was neither of his parents: it was his grandmother Rose Corre Isaacs.

Rose came from a rich family of Sephardic Jewish Portuguese – Dutch diamond dealers. A Sephardic Jew followed the customs and traditions of the Jews who originally lived in the Iberian Peninsula. After they were expelled from Portugal in the 15th century, a large community settled in Amsterdam.

Rose's folk were very strict Jewish-Victorian people, and the youngster rebelled against them. She had pretensions to be an actress but never made the big time, so, instead of treading the boards, she created her own world that would have made a book in itself.

Ensconced in a beautiful house in London's Highbury, a free-kick from the old Arsenal stadium, Rose filled it with a varied selection of luvvies, bohemians and homosexuals. A frequent visitor was crime writer Agatha Christie. She did not get on with her husband, a master tailor by trade, and banished him from the marital home. He ended up living a few streets away, Rose adding insult to injury by refusing to adopt her married name. That was her way of dealing with things.

Rose had more schemes for making money than Arthur Daley and, like the *Minder* character's ducking and diving, many of her plans were illicit. One of them involved selling fake paintings. Dowdily dressed in some of her old theatrical clothes, she would tour the great houses of London pretending to be down on her luck, having fled Europe because of the war and now compelled to sell these beautiful Victorian paintings. When Rose died, among her possessions was a collection of fakes done by a friend of hers.

Another wheeze involved stealing cars and renting them out on the lucrative black market that had sprung up during the war. Peter McLaren's services as a driver were required for this operation and, despite the fact that she had a deep-rooted hatred of him, Rose employed him. She even let him hide out in her cellar as he was on the run from the army, when the young Peter did not fancy his chances fighting in the war.

Eventually, when the car business wound down, she paid him off just to disappear. Peter McLaren took the money and ran. He dropped off the radar completely and McLaren did not see him again for over 40 years. Deprived of a father figure in his life, the youngster was soon to all but lose his mother, too. Emily hated motherhood and effectively left her sons for Rose to bring up. This rejection had a tremendous effect on McLaren, shaping his whole life.

Although she lived next door, Emily became like a stranger to her son. He compared her once to an older

3

sister that had gone strange. McLaren told Ginny Dougary in a *Times* interview: 'My mother might as well have been a stranger, or a sort of strange aunt who visited once a week.

'The effect of growing up in a family that never wanted to be a family is that it is very difficult for you to behave in a normal way, to respect any form of authority. I think, if you have clear parental figures in your life, you get to know at a very early age who to listen to and who not to listen to and how to behave.'

So the way was clear for Rose to mould McLaren into the figure she wanted to be herself. Almost a Frankenstein situation, Mary Shelley's Gothic novel was one of Rose's favourite books. As Martin Amis once said, 'One reaches for one's Penguin Freud.'

It is interesting to compare McLaren's unconventional childhood with that of John Lennon, perhaps the greatest pop star this country has produced. Lennon was brought up by his aunt Mimi, and for years thought that his mother Julia was his older sister.

Rose had been repressed and constrained by her Victorian parents, forced to conform. Now she effectively taught her grandson to reverse the normal moral code, wanting him to challenge authority when he came up against it. Rose also brought him up to criticise the establishment. She had a deep-rooted loathing for people who lived in a certain way and indoctrinated the youngster with maxims that he later incorporated into his own personal manifesto:

1) 'The English are a nation of liars and the Royal Family is its symbol.' (This might explain a lot why McLaren found himself sailing on the Thames that night on the *Queen Elizabeth*. Also why he was the man that was responsible for selling the image of the Queen with a safety pin through her bottom lip.)

2) 'To be good is bad.' That phrase was to haunt McLaren for the rest of his life.

3) Rose loved chaos and discomfort: when people were uncomfortable, that was when she thought that they really revealed themselves. 'Cash from Chaos' was one of the slogans that McLaren used in the Sex Pistols film *The Great Rock'n'Roll Swindle*. The only clothes he admitted to have made for a specific purpose was a tartan bondage suit for his appearance in the movie. Under the suit he sported a T-shirt with the motto spelled out in large white suede letters.

Rose set about educating her grandson from a very early age. She was totally focused on McLaren to the exclusion of his older brother Stewart. Almost completely ignored by his grandmother, Stewart started staying out late and eventually dropped out of school at 15. Rock'n'roll had arrived in the UK, and like a lot of young men at that time Stewart became a disciple. It was about to sweep aside a lot of values, musical and otherwise.

5

Rose drove a wedge between the two brothers, refusing to let them share a room or bond in any manner. That was how she ran the family, dividing to conquer, ignoring those who were of no use or interest to her. The treatment of McLaren was totally different as she tried to dominate him completely, ensuring that he could build no proper relationships with anybody else. It was a claustrophobic, stifling experience that led to some deep-rooted issues. She would read to him for hours at a time: among the books were *Oliver Twist* and *A Christmas Carol*. Rose loved Charles Dickens and the imagery of his work was to influence McLaren greatly, particularly true of his work in the Sex Pistols film.

She hired a tutor for McLaren who taught him to read *Jane Eyre*. He learned quickly but was on record as saying that he hated the book so much he was put off reading for life. At his first day at school (and his last if some interviews are to be believed), he was given a 'Peter & Jane' book to read and was deeply upset.

When he was six, McLaren's mother remarried a man called Martin Levi who owned a clothes factory in the East End and a string of shops. The factory was called Eve Edwards London Ltd and McLaren later temporarily adopted 'Edwards' as his surname, his rejection of the McLaren name another protest against his parents' treatment of him.

One of Emily's boyfriends before her marriage to Levi

had been Charles Clore, who bought the Selfridges store in London's Oxford Street. McLaren always had a fascination with the area and later made a film about it. All his family had connections with the rag trade so it was not surprise that eventually he opened a clothes shop himself.

Rose absolutely refused to send him to school and kept him at home receiving private instruction until he was ten, but eventually the boy attended a school on Stoke Newington Church Street in North London, which is now a block of trendy flats. In interviews he would always say that he could never accept a teacher but for a while he went to school like a normal child. The problem was he never behaved like one; he had no interest in sports and joked that the only pet he ever owned was a cockroach.

At school McLaren was quickly identified by teachers as a disruptive force, a troublemaker from a broken home, Rose's subversive teachings already awakening something inside him. Every classroom has one, and soon he began to coerce and coax his classmates into all sorts of mischief. All boys like to be in gangs and one sunny afternoon he lured some of his partners in crime to a nearby rubbish tip and made them enter a large cardboard box that had been discarded there. McLaren was forming his first gang – 'The Box Gang'. It was borne out of his youthful loneliness.

McLaren never learned the social skills most boys acquire at school, regarding his classmates as imbeciles because they lacked the intellect and confidence already instilled in him by his eccentric grandmother. He always went his own way with his own code of conduct built upon a feisty, nose-thumbing defiance of society's rules and conventions.

His childhood was generally unhappy and confused. His son Joe Corre once told a story that McLaren had ended up in a home for a few days after he'd been ill in hospital and nobody had come forward to claim him.

On a BBC2 tribute to McLaren, *Artful Dodger*, his partner Young Kim explained that in the last few years of his life McLaren was haunted by anxiety dreams about his early childhood, particularly the formative years of two to nine concerning food and clothes.

There were rare moments of normality, of course. McLaren once told *The Jewish Chronicle* that one of his happiest memories was reading their paper in his grandmother's front room.

McLaren's bad behaviour continued, causing mayhem at classmates' homes and disorder in the classroom. It was probable that he caused problems in his friends' homes out of envy of the fact that he did not have a proper one. The headmistress would summon Rose to her study from time to time to demand assurances about the future behaviour of the problem child. McLaren described the scene to Ginny Dougary in *The Times*: 'My grandmother was extremely possessive and forbade me to have anything to do with girls from the age of 13, but, if I was the worst-behaved person at a friend's house or causing tremendous problems at school, that was all fine.

'She would go to the headmistress and say, "Boys will be boys. What's wrong with what he does? If he drives me crazy I just bash him with my handbag. So I don't know what your problem is."'

McLaren made a mental note of the 'boys will be boys' phrase: it covered a lot of eventualities. As the situation deteriorated at school and the authorities became alienated by Rose's attitude and barely concealed contempt, they were keen to send young Master McLaren to a special-needs school, and Rose, realising the gravity of the situation, acted quickly by withdrawing him from the school and ordering more home tutoring.

This had the effect of making McLaren even more isolated from normal life and drew him even closer to his extraordinary grandmother. Years later, he said that he gave up art and painting to 'mould people' instead, clearly a reference to the Sex Pistols. Rose had attempted the same thing with him. She started encouraging him to wear girl's clothes and grow his curly locks even longer, almost a Pre-Raphaelite look, like the paintings that she had once sold imitations of.

Rose also shared a bed with McLaren, who was then about 14, although he always vehemently denied that there was anything sinister in it, insisting that it was just part of her controlling behaviour. Which might be a good time to clear up McLaren's sexuality. Many cynics saw the early relationship with John Lydon as being homosexual. Lydon always denied this, telling the *Observer* in 1994: 'Did I fancy Malcolm McLaren? Oh no, no – heheh. It's very fashionable to think that I was gay. I'll deny nothing. It is all talk. I don't care what you call me. I'm rotten to the core.'

Ari Up, singer in The Slits punk group (whose mother Nora later married Lydon), had a different take on McLaren. In an interview with Simon Reynolds for his *Totally Wired* book, the author asked her if McLaren was sexist. (There was a lot of speculation at one point that McLaren would take over management of the group and turn them into a female version of the Sex Pistols.)

Ari's response was: 'He was sexless. Not homosexual, not straight.'

Lauren Hutton, the gap-toothed actress (*American Gigolo*, *Lassiter*) and model, would disagree. In the mid-'80s, McLaren had a tumultuous affair with her after a chance meeting in a car park outside a restaurant in Beverly Hills. Legend has it that Hutton seduced him by surrounding herself with a bed of flowers outside his apartment door. In a space of 24 months Hutton had appeared on the front page of *Vogue* a record 14 times. After she'd learned of McLaren's dubious childhood, she remarked that it was surprising that he did not end up a serial killer. (Ted Bundy, America's most infamous serial killer, was born the same year as McLaren.)

Unquestionably McLaren was seriously damaged by his childhood but it propelled him on to some truly astounding achievements. By any reasonable criterion, he was extraordinarily complex. Curiously enough, the *Daily Mirror*'s most famous agony aunt, Marjorie Proops (born Rebecca Marjorie Israel), was given her opportunity thanks to the sponsorship of Rose, who had paid for her education at Hackney Art College and also found her initial job on the *Mirror* as a fashion correspondent. It was a pity that Proops could not have given some counselling to McLaren as his teenage years grew increasingly fraught.

He was spending more time with Emily and his stepfather. Unfortunately, they didn't get on. Emily, no docile housewife, was keen for McLaren to get a job and sent him to the local labour exchange (now called Job Centres). In those days, there was work for young people and he was offered gainful employment at Sandeman, the port and sherry merchants in Piccadilly. The wage offered was £6.50 per week. McLaren told *Loaded* magazine, 'My mother, being a terrible snob, decided this was the job for me. I arrived in the morning,

I was blindfolded and I'd have to taste these little test tubes full of a whole variety of wines.'

The problem was McLaren did not arrive on time in the mornings and he was soon dismissed. Emily was bitterly disappointed at his sacking as she had conventional ambitions for her son, of his maybe going into the fashion business. His next and final 'normal' job was working in a ballpoint-pen factory. McLaren's job was to recycle the plastic tubes that housed the pen by grinding them down into dust and putting them back into the moulding machine. He soon became incredibly bored looking at the transparent crystal plastic and started to experiment.

This involved him mixing dirt into the dust in the hope that it would throw up some speckled plastic instead. It failed to produce the desired result, however, and instead seriously jammed up the machinery. The owner of the factory was disgusted at McLaren's behaviour and he was sacked on the spot.

And so ended his dalliance with normal society. One of McLaren's proudest boasts was that he never filled in forms of any kind, from job applications to census forms. How many people can say that?

What was going to be his next move? He was at a crossroads with his whole life in front of him. He described the moment to *Loaded*: 'After I was fired I realised that I was destined never to fit in, to become a

'60s wild child, to remain unemployable, and act in the kind of way that suggests no fear of never having a career… difficult to sustain over a long period of time, particularly in the pragmatic world we live in today. But I don't think I'd have it any other way. My grandmother always had that attitude.'

CHAPTER TWO

SOMETHING ELSE

'When I was finally kicked out of art school after eight years, all I said was, I have to figure out how to become an excellent failure, how to create disasters.'
MALCOLM MCLAREN

'I think that it is a good thing for anyone to be, a brilliant failure. I can't stand success.'
LEONARD COHEN

Malcolm McLaren decided to go back to his studies and enrol in an art school. Once again, his grandmother was instrumental in his making the key decision. Inspired by her imagination and attitude, McLaren was determined to imitate her lifestyle and outlook on the world. In his words, he wanted to 'discover a new way of looking at life and then put it into practice'.

For the next eight years in the '60s and early '70s, he went on an odyssey through the outlying suburban art institutions in the South of England.

Jumping forward almost a quarter of a century to the early autumn of 1988, McLaren received one of the biggest honours of his career, a retrospective in a museum called 'Impresario: Malcolm McLaren and the British New Wave', staged at the New Museum of Contemporary Art in New York City, in the shadows of the Twin Towers.

The exhibition consisted not of sculptures or paintings but:

Posters (including the one for the Summer Rock Festival in July 1976 held at the Lyceum and attended by a 18-year-old Paul Weller who had just formed his own band, The Jam)
Flyers (including one for the Screen On The Green Midnight Special where The Clash made their London debut)
Stencilled T-shirts (including one bearing the logo 'Too fast to live, too young to die', and featuring the skull and crossbones)
Other garments made during his relationship with Westwood (including the Anarchy Karl Marx shirt considered to be the definitive statement by the pair. McLaren was later buried near Karl Marx in Highgate Cemetery)
Record Covers (including the picture cover for 'Pretty Vacant', Jamie Reid's most rushed piece of

*artwork, quite literally thrown together on the way
to Virgin Records. It featured the situationist buses
design)*

The list is long, but there was just one small artefact
from McLaren's eight-year stint in the art schools, a
painting with the statement: I will be so bad.

In 1963, he joined his first art school, St Martins
College of Art in Charing Cross Road. This was also to
be the scene of the first gig that the Sex Pistols played in
central London a dozen years later. It was while he was
working at Sandeman that he stumbled across St
Martins, as he explained to *Swindle* magazine: 'On our
way to lunch me and the other boys would often pass
this doorway where the best-looking girls entered,
wearing fishnet stockings and overgrown woolly
sweaters with long hair and dark mascara eyes. It was a
place called St Martins Art School.'

In his personal life, another huge change had
occurred: he had discovered rock'n'roll. Some time
later, during his time in the art schools, though, he
appeared to have acquired a sudden dislike of popular
music and all its trappings. At the height of punk, he
showed utter disdain for rock or any type of popular
music, claiming his only interest in it was as a force
for change.

One of his tutors, art historian Theodore Ramos,

explained to his students that 'Musicianship was for the more stupid kind of artist'. Perhaps he had Sid Vicious in mind when he made this statement.

This dislike varied from the experiences of his early days in connection with music. The first real exposure to rock'n'roll came at a Christmas party in his first year at his grammar school, Whitechapel Foundation. An older pupil came on stage and sang a rousing version of Jerry Lee Lewis's 'Great Balls Of Fire'.

McLaren had never seen anything like it and started to read up about Jerry Lee's mercurial rise to fame and his audacious personality. Before his career came crashing down as a result of his marriage to his 13-year-old cousin, Jerry Lee was the only artist to ever threaten Elvis Presley's place as the undisputed king of rock'n'roll.

It was thanks to his brother Stewart that his first visit to a concert gave him the opportunity of seeing two of the greatest rock'n'roll stars of all time: Eddie Cochran and Gene Vincent. But tragedy was to follow and obliterate their talent.

One of McLaren's obituaries made reference to the fact that he had seen Buddy Holly at the Finsbury Park Astoria (later known as the Rainbow) in 1960, when Holly had already been dead for a year. At that time, the BBC Light Programme was the only station that played pop music of any sort. Television was just as restricted, with pop music only featured early on Saturday night: David Jacobs in *Juke Box Jury* on BBC, followed by *Boy Meets Girls*, hosted by Marty Wilde on ITV. McLaren would try to catch Wilde's show, which is where he first saw Gene Vincent and Eddie Cochran.

The story of Eddie Cochran was one of great unfulfilled promise. Strikingly handsome, he bore a remarkable resemblance to James Dean. Tragically, both men died in car accidents. The rebellious handsomeness, rockabilly leather jacket and swept-back hair gave him an iconic image that is still fashionable today. Comparisons with Elvis were always being made, but Cochran held an advantage over Presley in that he wrote his own material and insisted on complete control in the recording studio, almost unheard of at that time. Elvis was essentially a singer of other people's songs, whereas Eddie was an innovator.

The latter was a great influence on McLaren, especially the clothes and the independent image. Seeing Cochran live turned his head completely. The near-hysterical audience was mostly comprised of Teddy Boys and the look was to stay with McLaren for the rest of his life, particularly one Ted in an electric-blue drape-jacket suit and the obligatory thick-soled brothel creepers on his feet. Boy, fancy wearing a suit like that – people would certainly notice you, an idea that greatly appealed to the young McLaren.

The show was promoted by impresario Larry Parnes, at the time the most famous and powerful manager in British pop music. One of Larry's future stars on the bill that night was a precocious 16-year-old called Clive Powell, playing in Cochran's backup band. Soon Clive was to change his name to Georgie Fame (a name that seems to get better over the years). Fame's music was the place where black and white music met, his unique blend of blues and jazz ensuring a career of great longevity. At the time of writing, Fame was enjoying a week's residency at Ronnie Scott's legendary club in Soho.

That night a fight broke out in the stalls and soon spilled into the street. 'Teddy Boys will be Teddy Boys', to paraphrase his grandmother. The Teds were hard nuts, as the Mods and later the punks were to find out.

The show had a special kind of excitement that provoked a type of hysteria previously unknown in the UK. In subsequent years, the breakthrough of The Rolling Stones and The Beatles produced similar scenes, but at that time it was a completely new phenomenon.

Eddie Cochran first appeared on stage with his back to the audience, and when the band kicked into 'Something Else' he whirled around strumming his famous orange Gretsch guitar. The effect was devastating and the audience literally went berserk. McLaren was quick to spot the effect such behaviour could have on people.

On *The Great Rock'n'Roll Swindle* soundtrack album, two Cochran songs were used: 'Something Else' and 'C'mon Everybody'. By that time, the Pistols had fragmented under the weight of the different personalities in it, with Lydon having quit. 'Something Else' was put out as a single in February 1979, 22 days after the death of Sid Vicious. Cartoon stills were used from the movie to promote the track. Nothing new in that.

A few weeks after the London show, Cochrane was killed when his privately hired taxi crashed into a lamppost, throwing Eddie through the windscreen. The 21-year-old died from his head injuries the next day. Gene Vincent, also travelling in the car, survived the crash but his health was never the same and he died in 1971 at the age of 36 from a ruptured stomach ulcer. Both men became deities in the world of pop music. Too fast to live, too young to die.

The taxi driver was later jailed for six months for dangerous driving. As Cochran lay dying in hospital, Parnes was already switching a song called 'Three Steps To Heaven' from the flip side that it was already slated to be. Subsequently released as the A-side of a single, the record soared to No 1 in the charts. McLaren was quick to see the implications of Parnes's move. Tony Wilson, the Manchester-based TV presenter turned head of Factory Records, was accused of acting in a similar manner when the Joy Division singer Ian Curtis hanged himself. But Wilson always denied cynically hustling Curtis's sublime song 'Love Will Tear Us Apart' – while the cover which featured a tombstone, it had been chosen and the single released before his death.

Over the next few years, McLaren was to see both the fledgling Stones and Beatles play live in London before they became famous worldwide. Eventually, they got bigger and bigger and took over the planet. Inspired by the vision of Eddie Cochran, McLaren began to frequent Soho, in those days the most happening place in the world. Rock'n'roll acted as an amphetamine on him, and he became a regular at the fashionable 2i's coffee bar in the basement of 59 Old Compton Street, where Cliff Richard, Joe Brown and Tommy Steele were all discovered and got their first break in show business. The complete list of stars who performed there is really a who's who of English rock'n'roll.

The place was packed out with heartbreakingly beautiful bohemian-looking girls and young hustlers like him. A young fellow called Lionel Bart had once played the washboard in a skiffle group there. Now he was the toast of Broadway and earning £16 a minute from his smash hit *Oliver*. There was a rumour that McLaren had once been employed by Bart as a driver. Another turn at the Coffee Bar was Paul Gadd who later changed his name to Paul Raven and then, eventually, to Gary Glitter. Both men courted their own ruination, Bart through drink and drugs, and Gadd through his sexual appetite for young girls.

There was a restaurant in Soho called Bianchi's that McLaren sometimes visited, which did a very reasonable spaghetti Bolognese. Terence Stamp used to frequent it a lot in the late '50s. Cat Stevens' parents ran a restaurant called the Moulin Rouge at the North End of Shaftesbury Avenue, close to Sandeman in Piccadilly. The Cat was born Steven Georgiou, son of a Greek-Cypriot father and Swedish mother. Like McLaren he had a difficult upbringing too; his parents split up when he was eight, and his early school days were lonely and troubled.

Stevens later joined the Hammersmith School of Art, where he turned to music playing in the local coffee houses and pubs. He later became a Muslim and changed his name to Yusuf Islam, but in between became one of the most successful singer-songwriters of all time.

Although he was broke most of the time and barely able to afford the price of a cappuccino in the coffee bars, other McLaren haunts of the day were La Discotheque and a club called the Saint Germain De Pres in Poland Street. His head was full of schemes and dreams and as he caught the night bus home he mulled them over, wondering which, if any, would come true.

Even in his wildest dreams, he would have found it

hard to believe that a decade and a half later the club would be called Louise's and act as the epicentre of the emerging punk scene, for which he claimed responsibility. Louise's was named after its owner, and McLaren recounted the story of his return there to the *NME*: 'There was Louise sitting by the door in her mink stole, the same woman who I knew from those days, charging 50p entrance. And when Anarchy was released there was champagne.'

At that time, Louise's was a lesbian club that was 'rediscovered' by Siouxsie Sioux and soon to be the hangout for most of the major punk bands. After a few years, it changed hands again and became Toppers Wine Bar, before becoming a lap-dancing club.

McLaren's best friend at the time was one Bernie Rhodes, later manager of The Clash, who he met at a bowling alley on Stamford Hill. Bowling alleys were great meeting places for the youngsters and it soon became a stamping ground for the burgeoning Mod culture that was rapidly spreading in the early '60s. Rhodes grew up in the East End of London and went to school in Brixton, and, like McLaren, his ideas were formed from art, style, bohemia and literature. Bernie also had a difficult childhood.

Among the young, predominantly Jewish mods who hung around the bowling alley was Mark Feld, later to be known as Marc Bolan. Marc was a rock'n'roll fan too: he had carried Eddie Cochran's orange Gretsch to his car that night at the Astoria. Coincidentally, Bolan was also killed in a car crash, in the momentous year of 1977.

Rhodes was no scholar, and he and McLaren spent most nights hanging around in Soho gazing in awe at the sights. McLaren's taste, meanwhile, had shifted from rock'n'roll to the newly happening R&B scene in London.

R&B in these times was different from the black soul music of today. Rod Stewart was singing with a band fronted by the late Long John Baldry. In the week the Pistols stormed the charts with 'God Save The Queen', the record they had to beat off the top spot was our little Rod the Mod's 'I Don't Want to Talk about It', a double A-side with a Cat Stevens song 'The First Cut is the Deepest'. It was particularly galling to McLaren that his creation was shown on the charts as being No 2 to the Stewart/Stevens effort, even though it sold more copies that week. With the song banned by the BBC, the establishment could not allow such an outrage as the Pistols having a No 1 in Jubilee week and the sales figures looked as if Stewart's record retained the top spot thanks to the spurious idea it had received a large number of advance orders. One of the few times McLaren had been swindled.

McLaren got his first glimpse of The Rolling Stones one sunny afternoon when he stumbled into a basement club in Newport Street. Playing a lunchtime session were the lads themselves, wearing leather waistcoats and long faces. McLaren preferred a band called The Pretty Things who had the longest hair of any group of the time. 'They were the most outrageous group in London, at the time, far more so than the Stones,' he told the *NME*.

McLaren was always big on outrage.

The Stones' manager, Andrew Loog Oldham, was a young guy wearing a sharp Italian three-button mohair suit and huge dark glasses. In the gloom the shades looked ridiculous.

Oldham's father had been shot down in a B-52 bomber shortly before his son's birth. He was another product of the Soho coffeehouse scene, a real hotbed of talent and ambition. (Peter Grant, the notorious manager of Led Zeppelin, started off in the music business as the bouncer at the 2i's. McLaren was fascinated by Grant and tried unsuccessfully to make a film about his life.)

A self-confessed hustler and huckster, Oldham was the prototype new breed of manager: hip, educated, beautifully dressed, ruthless and focused. Comparisons were constantly made between him and McLaren, and both were from the same mould that was for sure. Mentally, they were not too far apart at that time, and both were to eventually jump ship from their greatest creations to pursue their pranksterish ambitions.

One of Oldham's first ploys in the record business was to retain ownership of the Stones' master tapes and only lease them to their then record company Decca. This obviously gave the band greater clout and artistic licence. Phil Spector, currently serving 19 years to life in an LA prison for second-degree murder, had been the first manager to operate in this fashion.

Oldham was also promoting the Stones as the bad boys of pop as opposed to the (at that time) squeaky clean, wholesome loveable 'mop top' image that The Beatles represented. 'Would you let your daughter go out with a Rolling Stone?' was one of his slogans.

The Beatles' manager was Brian Epstein, a gay, Jewish-born entrepreneur, who wanted to package them for the mainstream market. McLaren saw The Beatles when they played their first gig in London in the Pigalle restaurant in Piccadilly. Rather predictably he was not very impressed by them.

'I was not knocked out by them. The main thing was that they sounded exactly like the record, we were not used to that. They were too cold, too unsexy.'

The Beatles were always regarded as being too provincial for the hip young things of London. To them the main difference between the bands was that The Beatles came from Liverpool and the Stones from the South. One of the reasons that Glen Matlock, the Pistols' original bass player, departed the band was that he was a Beatles fan, while McLaren often reminded us that he was 'anti-music'.

Ideas were already forming in McLaren's mind, always looking for a market for that androgynous, maverick, rebel image. Shortly before his death, McLaren was extolling the virtues of Pete Doherty, whose drug-fuelled exploits and relationship with model Kate Moss made him the most controversial pop star of the present day, Doherty had people dying all around him and had a tendency to drop wraps of drugs in court. Wonderful fodder for the tabloids. However McLaren stated that, 'He might just be the most brilliant apparition we have ever created.'

Before he got involved in the music business, though, McLaren was furthering his education. He always claimed that he had got himself sacked from Sandeman so he could enrol at art school. His first port of call after leaving St Martins was to enrol at his local art school in Harrow. In those days you could get into art school with scant qualifications, which was just as well for McLaren who had amassed a meagre two O Levels. Many of the '60s English rock-scene superstars originated from those institutions. Pete Townshend of The Who, Ray Davies of The Kinks and guitar hero Jeff Beck (later to work with McLaren) all took this path. A decade later, Queen's Freddie Mercury was also a product of Ealing Art College.

Rose was most displeased with her grandson's career change and was worried about his exposure to this different world. She was soon firing off a blistering letter to the principal at Harrow demanding in no uncertain manner that he be barred from drawing women in the life classes, both infuriating and embarrassing McLaren. He decided to leave home and break free from the clutches of his grandmother.

In *Swindle* magazine, he explained about the only thing he learned at art school: 'It was during the very first lecture I ever had, at the little art school in Harrow. This goatee-bearded brown-corduroyed guy walked in and said, "So I suppose you all think you are going to be successful painters, sculptors and graphic artists etc?"

'Everyone nodded their approval, because that is exactly what you want to hear on your first day. Almost within the same breath he turned around and said, "If any one of you here thinks you're going to be successful, there's the bloody door. Leave right now. What you all have got to understand now is that you are all going to fail."

'We had been in the school half an hour. A huge hush fell over the room, everybody's faces sank into their shoulders. And then he finally turned around and said, "You know failure's not such a bad thing." And that was it. One year passed. Many of us fell by the wayside. I barely survived. We were in the same room in our second year and the same guy comes in and says, "So you are still here then?"

'We nodded. "You are just beginning to understand what failure is. You understand the struggle. That's why you'll survive. And one more thing, don't think you can just 'fail'. Be a flamboyant failure. That is better than being any kind of benign success."'

This was an epiphany for McLaren, a light-bulb moment. If his grandmother's 'good is boring' was the mantra of his private life, then the 'flamboyant failure' was the riff that he carried into his professional career.

Another lecturer at Harrow was Sir Peter Blake, the legendary artist behind The Beatles' iconic *Sgt Pepper's Lonely Hearts Club Band* album cover. One day McLaren turned up at a lecture to find Blake playing a saxophone. When he enquired what he was doing, Blake replied, 'Painting.'

The fact that McLaren was being taught by a great artist like Blake was a testimony to the quality of the education system of the time and a wonderful example of the sheer talent the country had at its disposal in the '60s. McLaren would always take pains to state he was a product of that golden era.

McLaren continued his studies in the colleges, where little if anything had changed since the 1930s. At this stage, the art student had no intention of returning to the normal world, and in fact he never did. He even saw this period of his life as a political statement being made against society. Work to him now was 'like a visit to the dentist'.

The next whistle stop was South East Essex School of Art and then on to the Chiswick Polytechnic. Situated on the leafy Bath Road near Turnham Green, the poly was renowned for its high standards. McLaren did not fare very well and was expelled in 1966, but he was enjoying the time to experiment with his art. One of his notebooks at the time commented that: 'Frustration is one of the great things in art. Satisfaction is nothing.'

When Margaret Thatcher came to power, her government closed the old art colleges. Young people masquerading as students were thrown out on their ear. The tutors did not fare much better and our friend in the brown corduroy at Harrow would have been one of the first casualties. Thatcher had no time for 'failure', flamboyant or otherwise. The next generation following the 'war babies' spawned the likes of Damien Hirst and Tracey Emin (who attended McLaren's funeral in April 2010) who made millions in the art game even if they did not make it entirely respectable.

All the while, McLaren the cultural insurrectionist was already planning and plotting. Stealing ideas from anywhere and everywhere, chewing it up and getting ready to spit it back into the establishment's face. In the late '60s, he joined Croydon College of Art where he met Jamie Reid, who was to have a huge influence on his life and help steer his career in a different direction.

CHAPTER THREE

GUY DEBORD

'We have a world of pleasure to win –
and nothing to lose but boredom.'
FRENCH SITUATIONIST SLOGAN

'In the '60s everybody was supposed to step out and be
young, because to be young was to be noble, to be noble
was to be free. We all believed this. We really did.'
MALCOLM MCLAREN

McLaren met Jamie Reid at the Croydon College of Art in the second half of the '60s, and their friendship almost earned them a place in a mental hospital. Their partnership was to provide the imagery that dominated the pop-art culture for generations. McLaren was by now using the name Edwards, and had started the 'ducking and diving' which was the pattern for the rest of his life.

Born in 1947, the year after McLaren, Reid was the son of the City Editor of the long since defunct *Daily Sketch* newspaper. Reid's early childhood was spent in

Shirley, a suburb of Croydon, South London. Typical suburbia, which McLaren and the Pistols saw as their greatest enemy. It was the theme of much of Reid's work, the 1974 book *Leaving The 20th Century* being the best example.

'Funnily enough,' Reid told *The Face* magazine in the '80s, 'suburbia was a very interesting, exciting place in the '20s and '30s when it was conceived, because it gave everybody a bit of garden, gave everyone a bit of space and a bit of their own time. And I think after that first generation went it became a bit of a monster unto itself. You have only got to walk around the suburbs now and see the new post-war working class Thatcher voters there, the new generation of suburbia.'

Reid was another product of the grammar school system and was educated at John Ruskin Grammar before moving on to Croydon Art School. The young artist of agitation came across as a rather dour character in his early days at the college, wearing a very earnest expression and working very diligently. His only outlet seemed to be when he played the saxophone (badly) in the common room at lunchtime. That was where he met McLaren, who had just been chucked out of Chiswick Poly for creating mayhem.

McLaren was doing a vocational course in painting but was getting heat from the local authority because this was a course that did not readily qualify him for a grant. He enjoyed the course because there was not much teaching involved and he was left to come up with his own ideas. Chastened by his time at Chiswick, McLaren was very quiet in those days, keeping himself to himself. The only thing that drew attention to him was his attire: his usual mode of dress was a huge military coat, several sizes too big for him, worn in most weathers with a peaked cap. Underneath McLaren's arm was a rolled-up newspaper (never a red-top) and there was always a Woodbine cigarette dangling from his lips. His hair was mid-length with the tight red curls protruding from underneath his cap.

Robin Scott, who was to have a big hit in the '80s with a song called 'Pop Muzik' with the band M, was another student at Croydon who would sometimes hang out with McLaren and Reid. One day in class McLaren caused a stir by asking Scott if he was colour blind so intrigued was he by the combination of colours the other student was using. Scott, McLaren and Reid had a mutual interest in the obscure French Situationists and they did not stop frothing about the movement when they used to meet up in a tough pub at the back of East Croydon Station, which was used by the local postmen who worked in the nearby sorting office.

On Saturday mornings, they would go to the Surrey Street market, one of the most famous street markets in South London. Its West Indian food and cheap fruit made it good value for the impoverished students. There were also some interesting second-hand record shops there which McLaren frequently visited on the lookout for old rock'n'roll records. He said that his interest in the music of the day had ended when The Beatles hit the scene.

McLaren had an incredible thirst for knowledge. He considered himself a disenfranchised art student with aspirations to do something more than play chess better than Marcel Duchamp. The Vietnam War was at its height and McLaren attended some anti-war rallies. The abolition of military service in 1958 kept England out of Vietnam. As a result McLaren and the likes of John Lennon, Pete Townshend, and Eric Clapton were not dodging bullets during the most creative phase of their lives. At that time McLaren was still an enigma, smoothly successful on the outside but fumbling in his relationships and inept at ordering his emotions.

At the rallies, a hotbed of political thinking, he learned about some clandestine groups that were running about causing trouble. This grabbed his attention immediately because he always loved gangs and groups of troublemakers. This mob was special because they were described as being 'artistic, disorientated, and sartorially elegant, while smashing things up'. As a point of reference, imagine a combination of the notorious Chelsea Headhunters football hooligan gang, which was forming around the end of the '60s, with first-class honours degrees. In the early '70s, with the hooligan wars at their height, Chelsea fans on the rampage after their home games would often smash the windows of McLaren's shop. It was an obvious target and the fact that the ground was only a short walk away made it particularly vulnerable. In the mid to late-'70s, Chelsea were at the opposite end of the scale to the Premiership team of the 21st century, broke and in danger of relegation to the old Third Division. Their fanatical following had a fearsome reputation for violence and destruction, and the majority of the gangs were drawn from the local youths who lived in the nearby council estates. There was an element of chaos to it also which was of special interest to McLaren, which is when the concept of chaos was first seeping into his consciousness.

Toby Young and Julie Burchill started a magazine called *The Modern Review* in the late '80s. It was ahead of its time – as were most of McLaren's ventures in that period – and short-lived, but he gave a great interview to them about his involvement with the Situationist movement.

'Someone told me, "This group you are looking for will often wear black gloves. They are fairly well disguised and strange-looking people. They will not have any banners." I managed to pick up their pamphlets. One was called King Mob Echo and was printed up by an English affiliate of the Situationiste

Internationale. It was a Situationist newspaper and it led me to a shop called Compendium Books on Camden High Street. [In the spring of 2010 McLaren's funeral cortège would pass down Camden High Street on its way to Highgate Cemetery, past the place that had given him the idea for his most outrageous venture.]

'I came across some magazines that were immediately seductive.

'It was because of their covers, one cover was virtually aluminium, it was so shiny-purple even. Another was sandpaper, called *Memories* [by Situationist International founding member Guy Debord]. But inside they all had the words "Internationale Situationniste". They were all written in French and there was the odd photograph, which was the only thing I could understand.'

The sandpaper cover was created so it could destroy all the other books around it. (Author's note, we contemplated putting this tome in such a cover but Waterstone's/HMV were not keen on the idea. Could catch on though; watch the shelves.)

McLaren made his purchases and was on his way out of the shop when the assistant stopped him and asked him if he wanted to buy the contents of a large brown paper bag that he had pulled from under the counter.

The scene between McLaren and the guy in the bookshop was reminiscent of a scene from the cult TV show *Budgie*, starring Adam Faith, a former pop star.

Budgie's eponymous hero was a chancer extraordinaire who operated in the Soho area. One of his scams involved working in a sex/porn book shop run by the local spiv Charlie Endell.

The brown envelope offered to McLaren contained seditious pamphlets such as *Keep The Dialectic Open*, which included some pornographic drawings. Also featured was a mock picture-strip interview between the unlikely pairing of John Wayne and Brigitte Bardot, all about Situationism.

This pamphlet blew McLaren's mind. The mish-mash of pop culture and politics is commonplace today: if you want proof, just look at the propaganda for the 2010 election, studded with references to movies and songs. To McLaren, however, it all seemed so new, dangerously vital and, even more importantly, anarchic. He bought the lot and began devouring everything he could on the subject.

McLaren confessed that at the time he knew little and was in his words 'a complete barbarian'. In his art education so far, he had seen a couple of Matisse paintings and had been lucky enough to be taught by Peter Blake, but that was the extent of it. The call of the artist was still pulling him, though, and perhaps throughout his life he was to be the perpetual art student. Scarred by his early *Jane Eyre* reading experience, he was by no means well read. McLaren winced at the memories of his grandmother insisting that he kept a dictionary on his knee as he attempted to follow the plot, and his love of literature had soon withered on the vine. All that was to change.

Guy Debord's name came up in his research as a mysterious, shadowy figure. At that time there were no photographs available of the French Marxist. Little of his early life was known except that he was born in Paris in December 1933 and was raised by his grandmother. Where have we heard this before? A pattern was quickly to emerge.

Just like McLaren, Debord had a disturbed childhood and a disrupted education. Naturally bright, he was always in conflict with the authorities. It is not known if his grandmother told him that 'bad is good' or to challenge any form of authority, but it seemed more than likely.

Debord studied law at the University of Paris but soon dropped out to become a poet preaching revolution and an independent filmmaker. Not that anybody in Paris or the bohemian milieu that McLaren/Reid lived within ever saw any of his films. Heavily influenced by Karl Marx, Debord founded the Letterist International schism with Gil J Wolman. In the '60s, though, he formed the Situationist International group, which first drew him to McLaren's attention.

Situationism advocated provocative actions as performance art and political statements, including Detournement – which drew heavily on the traditions of

Letterism – and plans for a mass strike against the system as a protest against the decline in spirituality caused by economic forces. McLaren was soon never without a dog-eared copy of Debord's *The Society of the Spectacle*: a major part of its appeal to him was that no book could ever explain its true concept. As always the magpie McLaren could plunder what he liked from it, his agile mind creating whatever interpretation suited him.

In the later stages of his life, Debord's health declined as a result of his excessive, drink-driven lifestyle. The decay of Debord's body was paralleled by the decay of the culture that he was so keen to dismantle. He became very reclusive and introverted but continued to write and study theoretical analysis that became profoundly bleak. Wracked by pain, he committed suicide in 1994, shooting himself in the head. It has been suggested by some historians that Debord and his obscure Situationist group was directly responsible for the French student riots that brought France to a standstill in the early summer of 1968.

McLaren talked about Guy Debord to *The Modern Review*: 'His whole philosophy was completely different to anyone else's. This movement has no copyright on its publications. I began to think about ideas like the spectacle of the commodity, which I now realise is Debord's central idea, but which I could not understand at the time. But you thought that the time was now ripe for a kind of artistic purging (almost Red Guard style) of the decadent world we live in.

'I tried to put these Situationist ideas to the test, and some of those situations. I remember with charm, with a wonderful sense of euphoria, giving away Christmas presents in Selfridges, dressed up as Father Christmas. Making 29 Father Christmases. Everybody is Father Christmas.'

This was one of McLaren's favourite exploits, consisting of him and Reid bursting into the store in their Father Christmas outfits. They proceeded to the toy department where they handed out the expensive teddies and shiny model cars to the children. The security guards were amazed to see such a thing and in the attendant confusion the pair made good their getaway. McLaren's obsession with Selfridges never ended. Towards the end of his life he was to appear there again, not as Father Christmas but giving a lecture in their 'Celebration of Punk' and still displaying the grandeur of his vision.

Meanwhile, McLaren continued plotting and planning, dreaming of organising agitation on a large scale. Another scheme involved wrapping a brick in the style of Guy Debord, folding it in the glossiest, most expensive wrapping paper and then putting a beautiful bow on it. A tag was added with 'Magic's Back' scrawled on it with a thick marker pen.

'Then in the early hours of the morning, going to a local church and hurling it through the window for the priest to pick up the following morning.'

It is not known if he ever did this.

McLaren never met Debord but they once arranged a meeting. It was in the summer of 1977 and the 'God Save The Queen' furore was at its height. Out of the blue McLaren received a call from the Situationist supremo. It was a great surprise when Debord congratulated him on his success, and also for stealing his ideas. Debord regarded it as a huge compliment that his ideology had been used to get a record to the summit of the charts without its being played, by a group that had scarcely performed. The fact that it was a direct attack on the pinnacle of the establishment was the icing on the cake for him.

McLaren asked him if he was phoning from London, but Debord was calling from Paris. They arranged to meet the next evening in McLaren's then local pub, The Man In The Moon, a few yards from his shop and across the road from his other haunt, The Water Rat. Debord had very precisely requested that they meet at 9.30pm. McLaren agreed and the next evening he found himself sitting in the pub wearing a trench coat and reading *The Times*. He said that he felt like Humphrey Bogart in *Casablanca*. The movies were mixed up by McLaren: Bogart playing the part of private eye Philip Marlowe in

The Big Sleep was the anti-hero image he had in mind. Like all good Bogartian gumshoe movies, the hero gets stood up and, come 10.30, McLaren was still waiting. Just as he was about to leave, the door burst open and two young Frenchmen all in black burst in. One of the attractions to McLaren of Situationism was that Debord ran it like a cult, some covert operation, with purges and a sinister undercurrent of paranoia. The youths headed straight for McLaren and sat down by him and start interrogating him with a fusillade of questions.

Who was he?

What right did he have to interfere with the work of Debord?

What role did he play?

What were his future plans?

When required, McLaren could use his tongue as a whip to cut down any opponent who threatened him. Perfectly delivered in his best icy Noel Coward tone, McLaren replied that he would not answer any questions until Mr Debord arrived. Paranoia was rife and McLaren enquired as to what time they could expect the great man.

'We are very sorry, Mr Debord goes to sleep at 9.30.'

That was the last and only time McLaren had any dealings with him. Debord's whole career was an enigma, and he was one of the greatest but least-read of the influential French writers. Debord's paranoia, whatever its origin, led him to imagine conspiracies that he came to believe. The line between deception and self-deception seemed blurred, leading his subordinates (the guys in the pub) to act like that. This book is about bamboozlers; there was no way McLaren and Debord would ever meet. What can be true in a world made up of forgeries, misappropriations, frauds and fakes? The painter who did not paint meeting the filmmaker who made movies no one saw.

McLaren was also fascinated by the painter Andre Daumier, a 19th-century caricaturist noted for drawing court scenes in a comical fashion. Controversial at the time, he was run out of town for his satirising and Daumier spent time on the run as the authorities tried to hunt him down. When the Third Republic was proclaimed, he was honoured for his work but immediately he was liked he became useless. As soon as he was loved, he lost his edge, his spark. A point that did not escape McLaren: it was important to know when to quit, timing was everything.

By this time, he had hooked up with the King Mob and became friendly with a chap called Christopher Gray. One of his ideas was to manufacture a 'totally unpleasant' pop group, vulgar, crude, hostile and totally anti-music. Almost The Monkees in some parallel universe. The concept appealed to McLaren and he filed it away mentally for future use.

The 'politics of boredom' was a constant refrain of his; he explained the concept in *The Modern Review*: 'They sell you back your ideas, sell you back this enormous selection of commodities, sell you back these cheap holidays in other people's misery. [The theme of a future single.] The cynic within us had discovered the fact that BOREDOM was an intrinsic ingredient in all of this. So how can we solve the politics of boredom, our boredom?

'A boredom that we felt the world was asking us to buy into through its commodities.'

It was boredom that drove the student to organise a sit-in at Croydon College in the summer of '68. In a fever of designer conceptualism, McLaren, assisted by his accomplices Reid and Scott, decided to test the parameters of the system at Croydon. They felt that the role of the teachers (of which artist and TV personality Barry Fantoni was one) was superfluous. Inspired by events on the other side of the channel, McLaren orchestrated a sit-in at the college's annexe at South Norwood.

Barricading themselves in, they bolted up the doors and issued a manifesto, a dangerous blend of arrogance and stupidity. Their demands were not very far-reaching, mainly personal beefs with the teaching staff, and it was all very parochial. It made *The Times* but the sit-in lacked any cohesion and soon petered out. When the holidays arrived, nobody wanted to be stuck inside a building in South Norwood. What did Eddie Cochran sing about the 'Summertime Blues' that night in Finsbury Park?

McLaren and Reid were in deep trouble. They had no interest in representing the students' interests or even entering into any meaningful dialogue with the powers that be. McLaren knew that his time was up in Croydon and he should move on. In June 1968, he and Reid took off for France to visit the battlefields of the riots. They had just missed the demos caused by the student unrest the previous month but it was still an exciting period of history and the first time that he had visited Paris. He had a love affair with the city for the rest of his life.

'Very positive,' Reid told *The Face* in relation to his feelings about the riots. 'They were about people taking control of their own situations and it had a tremendous sense of excitement, and a tremendous humour. There was a sense of moving forward then, of getting to terms with yourself and enjoying every day.'

The effect it had on McLaren was that he felt he should do something in his own country to shake up the world. Gil Scott Heron, then being touted as a 'black Bob Dylan', had advised us that the 'revolution will not be televised' but McLaren had other ideas,

Various histories of punk rock culture have hinted that McLaren's stay in Paris at the time of the student unrest was one of the many myths that he spread about himself. John Lydon was highly contemptuous of the whole business, always expressing surprise that a European art movement had galvanised a youth culture. Although the extent of McLaren's involvement (if any) with the events are vague, there is no doubt that it did leave a mark on him. It gave him an edge over his contemporaries. There were rumours that the pair had an association with the University of Nanterre-based Mouvement du 22 Mars (Movement of 22 March), producing slogans and posters.

The students in Paris had stood shoulder to shoulder with the striking Renault car workers, joined by anarchists, insurgents and the usual wave of petty criminals and hooligans. It was a source of amazement to McLaren that all these factions could become unified in a common cause. It was the students who had emerged as the real winners, however, as they were becoming citizens and they could now say what they what they wanted to be taught and in what manner. McLaren loved the fact that things were changing and a new challenge was coming.

He saw many slogans during his time there but among the ones that resonated with him were: 'Be reasonable – Demand the impossible' and 'Under the pavement lies the beach'.

Upon his return to England, the pin-sharp McLaren quit Croydon, to the annoyance of both Scott and Reid, and joined Goldsmiths College. The members of Britpop band Blur were educated there in more recent times, but when McLaren joined it was the time of Daniel Cohn-Bendit (one of the principal leaders of Mouvement du 22 Mars) and Tariq Ali, both fierce critics of the British Establishment in their day.

McLaren had no interest in painting pictures for money; he was just developing his other talents and trying to expand his horizons. The three years at Goldsmiths enabled him to pursue his other interests and gave him enough confidence to eventually open his own clothes shop. McLaren was not a great intellect and in the debates at the student union he used to couch his contributions in basic terms.

The first festival to be held at Goldsmiths was organised by him. At the end of three years, he suddenly quit without taking his diploma. Rose grudgingly accepted his dropping out of art school. By this time, however, he was in a relationship – arguably the most important relationship of his life – and his girlfriend Vivienne Westwood was expecting his child.

CHAPTER FOUR

VIVIENNE WESTWOOD

*'When we were young and I fell in love with Malcolm,
I thought he was beautiful and I still do. I thought he was
a very charismatic, special and talented person.'*

VIVIENNE WESTWOOD

*'[Vivienne] is a wonderful person, a brilliant craftsman.
London people are not craftsmen; they are very lazy about
that. She comes from the Pennines, and she is one of
those hard rock people. She has the ability to be able
to live and survive in the woods.'*

MALCOLM MCLAREN

*'I remember Westwood, she looked gorgeous.
I was really attracted. She had blonde hair with
purple-pink lips. She looked great.'*

SIOUXSIE SIOUX

John Lydon's post-punk band Public Image Ltd (or PiL) had their biggest hit single with 'This Is Not A Love Song', which reached No 5 in 1983. Inspired by a line from a song by their label mates the Flying Lizards, it was seen as a cynical comment on the saccharine love songs popular at the time. It could easily have been the theme song for the relationship between McLaren and Westwood. A sort of post-punk 'Our Song'.

She was born Vivienne Isabel Swire in the village of Tintwistle, Derbyshire in 1941, six years before the birth of McLaren. At that time, Britain was at war and desperately fighting against the might of Hitler's forces. Her parents Gordon and Dora had married two years previously, at the start of the war. Her father left his job as a greengrocer to work as a store man at the local aircraft factory, which built bombers.

In 1958, the Swires relocated to Harrow, and Westwood enrolled at the Harrow School of Art. Although it was a few years before McLaren attended the same college, it was strange how their paths were to criss-cross before finally converging. Her chosen subjects were fashion and silver smithing, which she needed for her scheme to create her own range of jewellery. Westwood quit Harrow after a single term and dropped out. She could see no future for a young working-class girl from the North of England in the world of fashion, at that time a closed shop riddled with snobbery.

Having decided on a career change, Westwood enrolled at a teacher-training college and qualified as a primary school teacher. The world of fashion seemed to have been left behind. She did, however, maintain a stall on Portobello Road, selling her homemade jewellery. When she was 20, Vivienne met Derek Westwood, a young apprentice at the nearby Hoover factory. They were married in the summer of the following year, with Vivienne wearing her own wedding dress, albeit not as controversial as the one that was to appear in the first *Sex And The City* film that was associated with her. The following year, Westwood gave birth to a son, Benjamin. (Ben was present at the hospital in Switzerland when McLaren died: it was highly significant that both Westwood's sons were present.)

Her marriage to Derek was soon in trouble because of their different personalities, and Westwood left her husband shortly afterwards. She took refuge in a squat and around that time McLaren met her. He knew her brother well and McLaren was actually sharing a ramshackle house with him along with some American draft dodgers anxious to avoid a trip to Vietnam. The guys were having a good time, enjoying themselves and just existing, where nobody bothered anybody else.

McLaren explained the story to Jon Savage, who recorded it on his famous *England's Dreaming* tapes now preserved in Savage's archive held at Liverpool's John Moores University.

'She was running away from her husband, and she came to live in the house. I was studying music, believe it or not. And drama. My grandmother always had visions of my being an actor, and at a very early age, back in the mid-'60s. I think I had been to one art school before, for about three months (St Martins) and I lived in a hotel and my grandmother supported me. Basically I was going to continue being supported by my grandmother if I took the idea of drama seriously. So I enrolled at a drama school and there I also took piano lessons studying Bartok.

'I hated the idea that girls should come and inhabit this house. It was boys only as far as I was concerned, and girls coming in made it look all dreadfully slimy. I brought her to tears every single day and she had this little kid, which I always hated and loathed. I almost persuaded her to leave, but her Northern stubbornness defeated that end, and instead, three or four weeks later, I decided to feign sick [in order to get in her bed]. Curiosity, at the thought of being inside a woman's bed – even though I was 21.

'She was a school teacher and there was something harmlessly perverse about the whole notion, of this spoiled brat being in bed with a school teacher.'

Westwood immediately fell pregnant.

Interesting points arising from this:

A) McLaren's reference to her 'Northern stubbornness'. The fact that she came from 'up North' was a constant source of amusement to him. He would often mimic her Northern accent by speaking in a plodding Yorkshire brogue as effectively as he mastered the Jewish argot of his grandmother Rose.

As he matured, McLaren had more respect for Northerners, praising Damien Hirst, Pulp, Oasis, Goldie and Björk as 'salt-of-the earth Northern creatures'.

B) McLaren lost his virginity to Westwood. Considering the fact that he been on the beatnik trail and trawled Soho since he was barely a teenager, it substantiates Ari Up's assertion that he was 'sexless'. As to whether or not Westwood was McLaren's type is also open to speculation. He was on record discussing his favourite type of female: 'I much preferred the Matelot shirt and the girl with the black stockings and muddy green holey sweaters and strange eye makeup.'

C) The reference to his grandmother's vision of him as an actor was typical of her grandiose plans and hopes for him. She supplemented her income by giving elocution lessons, hoping to reprise in some small fashion her thwarted acting career. But McLaren's whole life was an act with him as the star and players like Lydon as the juvenile lead.

D) McLaren refers to hating both Westwood and her first son but in the *Daily Mail*'s obituary he was quoted as saying that, at the time, 'Westwood was astonishing. I thought she looked very beautiful and I thought the kid was adorable.'

Rose was horrified that McLaren had made a girl pregnant. McLaren said that she never really forgave him and gave him money for Westwood to abort the child. Her answer to any problem was throw money at it, the same as she did to McLaren's father. The abortion never took place, Westwood spending Rose's money on a cashmere twin set from Bond Street instead.

So Joe Ferdinand Corre was born, the Corre in honour of his beloved grandmother. Ferdinand was dropped somewhere along the way, but Joe went on to co-found the exotic lingerie brand Agent Provocateur. Only a son of McLaren's could have come up with such a clever name.

McLaren was absent for the birth of his son, and did not have a clue what to do with a new baby. Eventually, three days late, he turned up at the hospital where he incurred the wrath of the chief nurse on the ward: 'If you are the father, why are you so late? Are you a long-distance lorry driver or something?'

Looking down at his suede shoes, McLaren mumbled something. The only other thing he could recall about the birth was how big and healthy young Joe looked.

The absent father bit was unfortunately a familiar pattern throughout Joe's childhood. McLaren barely saw him when he was growing up. With his mother carving out a career in the fashion world, young Joe was sent to boarding school.

Speaking to Sean O'Hagan in the *Observer*, Joe explained, 'His real good fortune was finding my mum as a partner-in-crime, someone who believed in him and his ideas. She would have done anything for him and him for her. Together, they were unstoppable, his ideas, her designs.

'It was hard for me because he never wanted to do the emotional stuff that comes with being a parent. He ran away from it and I found that hard to take. But, you know, he had a messed-up upbringing and he just did not know how to do it. His mother rejected him so he was brought up by his grandmother who was a lunatic really.'

McLaren's brother, Stewart, had married by now. An interesting bond grew between the two siblings: Stewart had married the first real girlfriend he had known, while Malcolm had slept with his first girlfriend, impregnated her and ended up living with her for the next 15 years. The younger of the brothers created his own world, though, that he could rampage around in, while Stewart, who had the more straightforward upbringing of the two, had no such luxury, even though he had been allowed to run free in his days as a Teddy Boy. In those times, McLaren was under strict supervision from his grandmother. For example, she would only allow him to watch television for one hour a day.

Over the next three or four years, McLaren bounced back and forth between his 'lunatic' grandmother and the mother of his son. Westwood obtained a council flat in Clapham, on Nightingale Lane, opposite the Common. It was to be Westwood's home for almost the next 30 years. She continued to teach the infants at Brixton until 1971. However, her interest in fashion was rekindled by the presence of McLaren, and in the evenings she started studying it again, particularly the 17th- and 18th-century cloth-cutting techniques. That period of history was of particular interest to her and the dominant theme in much of her work.

For a while the couple had a stab at the straight life, with Westwood teaching and McLaren looking after the kids as best he could. Westwood was a good teacher with lots of new ideas, and would take her class of eight-year-olds to see movies like *The Battleship Potemkin*. Another of her treats was to take them on outings to see the countryside by bus. Sometimes he would accompany Westwood on her trips to the countryside with her class. Taking the 'townies' into the country was always an interesting experience. His grandmother had insisted that he should be a boy scout, though he hated the uniform. Some of the skills he learned there were invaluable as he lit a campfire and cooked sausages for the kids. Ging gang goolie.

On another occasion, Westwood sent McLaren and a very young Joe out to Clapham Common at night to pick dandelions. Armed only with a torch, their brief was to gather as many as they could to enable Westwood to make dandelion coffee, part of a macrobiotic diet that she insisted they try. What it tasted like was not recorded but McLaren came back with numerous scratches and a boil on his back.

Westwood's only hobby was gardening; she loved the open air and the relaxation. She hated television and never read newspapers; like McLaren's grandmother, she lived in her own world.

McLaren was surprised at Westwood's religious side. She taught at Sunday school, which he could never get his head around. Most of his associates were decadent and she was righteous, almost puritanical. Her parents were upright god-fearing folk and disapproved of their daughter marrying a Jew. To them he was a total alien who could have come from another planet as far as they were concerned, and they thought their daughter had been heinously corrupted.

What McLaren brought to the deal was that he could give her access to a world of culture hitherto unavailable. Westwood was a highly intelligent woman with an insatiable craving for more knowledge. McLaren saw them more as a team than anything. Like everything, he saw it in commercial terms.

The couple decided to work together in fashion and had their hearts set on a shop on the King's Road in Chelsea. It was the golden age of the King's Road as tourists flocked there. Mr Freedom had his shop there and it was known worldwide as the taste-making rock'n'roll city. With a child to support and his grandmother no longer willing to fund him, McLaren needed to make some quick money. Westwood quit her teaching job and McLaren bought a couple of Singer sewing machines.

At the time, 430 King's Road, London SW10 was run by designer and retailer Trevor Miles, and called Paradise Garage. It was situated at the far end of the King's Road, the opposite end from the more fashionable Sloane Square. The area known as World's End was just down the road and Chelsea Harbour was yet to be built.

McLaren would always make a story out of any incident. His version of how they actually came to take over the premises was explained to *Swindle* magazine: 'I made myself a blue suit, copying the cover of an old Elvis Presley record, and walked up and down the King's Road. But no one even looked at me!

'So eventually, after weeks, I was stopped by an American guy dressed completely in black who pointed to a little hole in the road and invited me in there to sell clothes. It was 430 King's Road.'

Exactly who the American in black was McLaren never explained. Perhaps it was Johnny Cash. But that would have been Cash from Cash, not Chaos. McLaren made Westwood learn how to cut trouser patterns to enable him to have the suit. It was a shining hour for him as he realised another of his dreams. Some evenings he would stroll up to Sloane Square eyeing all those beautiful continental women, not a care in creation.

The Elvis record that he copied the suit from was from the cover of an imported American album, the 1959 RCA release *50,000,000 Elvis Fans Can't be Wrong: Elvis Gold Records Vol 2* and the greatest hits of Elvis were to feature heavily in the new shop. McLaren installed a huge Wurlitzer jukebox he had purchased cheaply in the East End. All day long, he would crank out rock'n'roll. Later he would mix it up with classical music.

At first, though, McLaren and Westwood had a kind of wholesale Teddy Boy-gear business operating out of their back room in Clapham. There was a lot of '50s stuff there including records, magazines, postcards, furniture and all types of memorabilia. McLaren would go out scouring old junk shops and markets for gear; there were no car boot sales in those days. And definitely no eBay.

McLaren opened the shop as an act of revolt against the hippies. He hated anything to do with hippies and called them 'Hippos'. The soundtrack of Cochran, Vincent, Holly etc drowned out the rustle of kaftans and the clink of beads. Later, when the *Swindle* movie came out, he coined the famous slogan 'Never trust a hippie'.

The lack of involvement by the hippies in the 1968 Paris riots was another bone of contention to McLaren. Later dealings with Richard Branson were always guarded as he regarded the tycoon as having a hippie background. Perhaps it was the beard.

Westwood changed her personality when the business started. Still very matriarchal, she also became very competitive: she wanted to create things, instigate things, and detonate the fashion world.

In the early days of their relationship, McLaren was the nice Jewish boy from Harrow, running up a bit of schmatta, on the fringes of the rock business. Not a causer of cataclysms.

Westwood was the power behind him. Her clothes changed, too, from the hippie-Laura Ashley gear she wore when they first met to army surplus stuff. Gunslinger chic, more urban, worn with no small degree of sexiness. She was incredibly thin and seemed to exist on nothing but jasmine tea. The ideas that were to inspire a legion of fashion designers were soon to be unleashed on an unsuspecting world. 'The look of music, the sound of fashion' was her agenda.

Westwood's life reads like a novel written by Emile Zola. His heroine Therese Raquin, in the obscure, eponymous novel, was 'supremely dominated by her nerves and blood'. The docile Westwood was awakened by the arrival of McLaren in her life. Years later McLaren claimed, 'I think I was in love with her but I did not do it justice.'

McLaren needed money to finance the new shop

which he obtained when he sold cameras and equipment that had been loaned to him from local art colleges to shoot a film about Oxford Street. The concept of the film was to show how the façades of the shops had changed over the years. It was a very hard subject to make a film about and McLaren's lack of filmmaking experience was a big handicap. McLaren's friend, South African émigré Helen Wellington-Lloyd, assisted him as far as making the film was concerned, but she thought the finished product was too amorphous to ever give it a proper ending.

They both went to Goldsmiths College and Helen later appeared in *The Great Rock'n'Roll Swindle* movie at McLaren's request. When Helen, who was born with the congenital condition achondroplasia dwarfism, was introduced to McLaren's larger-than-life grandmother, she thought Helen was a small child. It must have been a scene worthy of inclusion in *Swindle*.

Helen always thought that McLaren opened in the King's Road because of his love of rock'n'roll, particularly his obsession with Eddie Cochran. The amazing shirts and bootlace ties Eddie wore in his all-too-brief life were of particular interest to him. McLaren believed that a fashion statement like a bootlace tie had served its apprenticeship, same as anything. Time served like Lacoste and Fred Perry.

The sharply dressed Teds were always looking for

action, unlike the hippies dossing about getting stoned. The King's Road was awash with drugs – chiefly speed – in those days, but McLaren was not interested in them. Perhaps that is why he had such an interesting career.

McLaren was lucky that, when the shop opened, there was something of a revival going in respect of rock'n'roll. In August 1972, Wembley hosted a sell-out revival show featuring Bill Haley, Jerry Lee Lewis and Little Richard. The Teds were out in force and they wanted to be wearing their best threads. A guy called Chinese Den actually made the Teddy Boy suits for McLaren. Westwood was now designing Zoot suits and peg-trousers to complement the drapes and drainpipe trousers.

There was a guy called Pete Meaden who was a Mod legend in 1964–65. McLaren used to hear his name spoken in awe around the coffee houses of Soho. He died at the age of 36 from a drugs overdose, forgotten, but his influence on modern culture should never be underestimated. He was best mates with the 'Ace Face' Phil The Greek, who appeared on the music TV show *Ready Steady Go* with a loaded shotgun. Meaden had seen the possibility of calculatedly making a band the apex of a youth revolution a dozen years before McLaren repeated the trick with the Sex Pistols.

The band Meaden styled was The Who, and without his input it is doubtful whether they would have made it, or even if the mod fashion would have spread so fast or even so far. He claimed that his major contribution was putting Roger Daltrey into a Zoot suit whose jacket had actual side vents five inches long. The band were then called The High Numbers, and Meaden wrote their first single, released on Fontana, 'I'm The Face' b/w 'Zoot Suit'. The original press handout designed by Meaden had a picture of Daltrey in the famous jacket, top button done up.

Later in the year, McLaren got a contract to make the costumes for Claude Whatham's rock'n'roll movie *That'll Be The Day*. It was the film that propelled David Essex to stardom, also featuring Beatles drummer Ringo Starr and Larry Parnes discovery Billy Fury.

Liverpool-born Fury was probably the best-looking pop star England ever produced. On a bad day he would still make James Blunt and co look like Carlos Tevez. McLaren always saw him as the English Eddie Cochran. Billy was to die from heart trouble. Dressed up in his Teddy Boy regalia for the film *That'll Be the Day* was one of his last moments in show business.

Robin Scott, McLaren's pal from Croydon Art College, also got involved with the shop. He had a car and he would drive McLaren up North looking for swag to offload in the shop. They were also looking for materials and fabrics that Westwood could use. Scott left after a while, claiming he could not live on the money that McLaren was paying him. Westwood implored him to stay, claiming McLaren was going to make him a partner, but it was too late.

Scott spoke on the *England's Dreaming* tape about the part Westwood played in proceedings. 'I always saw Vivienne as the woman behind the man. She was largely responsible for much of the drive and many of the ideas that McLaren had. They had a relationship that was about educating each other.

'She was doing all the bloody work back at the flat, and she knew she was holding it together. I admired Vivienne, I thought she was and still is a great person. Much more prepared to commit at an emotional level.

'She was happy for McLaren to be the centrepiece in the conversation when she had just as much to say.'

The growing reputation of the shop meant that soon a host of famous musicians were heading down the King's Road looking to improve their image. Among them were Iggy Pop and Ian Dury (who was rude to Westwood when she served him. Dury always claimed that he was the first person in London to adopt the safety pin as a fashion item). Other visitors were a group called The New York Dolls.

McLaren soon struck up a friendship with the group's founder member Sylvain Sylvain. They had walked in looking like a cross between The Rolling Stones and Lily Savage. McLaren was smitten and it was to have as big an influence on him as Guy Debord had.

The hardcore Teds came down to the shop at first but they started to see that the clothes were created by McLaren and Westwood rather than being originals. He was still trading some interesting records though, including a lot of the old Sun label Elvis stuff which is priceless today.

Always ahead of the game, McLaren decided to switch the focus of the shop, and in 1973 he transformed it into another of his concepts: Too fast to live, too young to die. It was a phrase that he was literally to take to his grave. Nobody was really sure where it originated. A number of people thought it was to do with James Dean, and it was in the lyrics to an Eagles song called 'James Dean', on the 1974 album *On The Border*.

The new gear was more in a 'rocker' style, biker jackets with studs and zips, leather caps, thick studded belts and heavy boots. This alienated the Teds even more. And tensions flared. McLaren was starting to get annoyed at the Teddy Boys, and he started to dread Saturday when the troublemakers would come down.

Whilst studying at Goldsmiths College, the job to aspire to was either that of a window dresser or a clothes designer. With 430 King's Road and Vivienne Westwood, he could be both.

CHAPTER FIVE

430 KING'S ROAD

*'I have always believed that talent only truly emerges when
there is a cause, a cause which is governed by survival.
Both me and Vivienne were trying to survive in a shop.
We were creating fashion with no parallel and no
industry to be connected to. So from day one we never
thought in terms of commercial gain.'*

MALCOLM MCLAREN

*'He gave us a belief in ourselves, helped us be on some kind
of scene. And his shop was a magnet, a speed-dating base.
McLaren gave us some kind of spurious accessibility.'*

GLEN MATLOCK

There is a classic picture of the employees of 430
King's Road taken in 1974 and featured in *Satellite*,
a pictorial history of the Sex Pistols by Paul Burgess and
Alan Parker. It was also featured in the contact
magazine *Forum* and passed into punk iconography.
Vivienne Westwood is on the extreme right in the
photograph wearing a cocaine white shirt with a classic

situationist slogan stencilled on it: 'Be reasonable –
Demand the impossible'.

Westwood's hair is short and bleached white/blonde,
and she is wearing the purple lipstick that Siouxsie Sioux
liked so much.

Beside her is a girl called Jordan (not that one), but,
like Katie Price, one of the most photographed young
ladies of her day. This Jordan is not as photogenic as her
namesake but like her she is in a state of undress. Later
Jordan was to appear in a costume based on Britannia for
the poster for Derek Jarman's disturbing *Jubilee* movie.

Chrissie Hynde, founder of The Pretenders, former
wife of the man who wrote 'Lola' and 'Waterloo Sunset',
Ray Davies, is standing next to Jordan and giving the
finger to the camera. Hynde had recently quit the *NME*.

One of the two males in the photograph is Alan Jones,
a young gay buck soon to be arrested in Notting Hill
Gate for wearing the infamous 'Two Cowboys' T-shirt,
which featured the eponymous wranglers with no
trousers. McLaren and Westwood were later charged
with 'exposing to view an indecent exhibition'. Today an
original of that T-shirt would fetch a small fortune.

McLaren was always amazed that the things they made
would sell at all. He found it ironic that they now stood
as objects d'art in auction rooms and museums. Profit was
not a concern to him and he insisted that they only did it
to create something to 'rub up against the culture'.

Completing the photo are a young shop girl, called Danielle, of whom not much is known, and a West London drifter called Steve Jones. A self-confessed 'toe rag', Jones provided the direct link to the Sex Pistols.

McLaren is not in the picture, as he had gone to New York to work with The New York Dolls in the autumn of that year. Tired of the retro-trash of his cartoonish Teddy Boy clothes, he was seeking new directions and an outlet for his rising anger. It was a short, strange period for him but it was to have a huge effect on his destiny and change the history of England.

Just a few weeks before his departure, McLaren and Westwood changed the name of the shop once again. This time it was simply called SEX, huge pink letters screaming the name across the façade.

The theme of the shop was now bondage and sadomasochism, the hipster Teddy Boy threads banished completely. The couple's attempt to turn fetish wear into high-street fashion was starting. It was never really established how this came about. There was no evidence of either McLaren or Westwood ever really participating in that scene. In fact, there were some rumours that McLaren had decamped to New York because the first cracks were starting to emerge in his relationship with Westwood.

In February 2010, shortly before McLaren died, fashion designer Alexander McQueen committed suicide. Liberty reported a 1400 per cent rise in sales of his designs. The most popular item was his headscarf, now as ubiquitous as Burberry, depicting the elegantly morbid skulls that had become his trademark.

Like McLaren, McQueen had studied at St Martins School of Art. The East Londoner was the natural successor to Vivienne Westwood as the enfant terrible of British fashion, early on in his career causing outrage with revealing dresses and Bosnia-imaged fabrics, just as Westwood, three decades before, had cleverly mixed up brilliant tailoring with outrageous concepts. It was all in the stitching.

In an interview conducted in the '90s with the hugely talented writer Michael Bracewell, McQueen hinted at the problems that were already lying in wait for him. 'I hate the circles that I move in now. I really hate them, the insular people you meet. I am a great believer in honesty and I do not think that you ever find it in fashion. I find it hard that my work is coming into my private life now. I find people giving me dirty looks for no reason.'

What is sure, though, is that McQueen was a true artist, like Vivienne Westwood: uncompromising, decades ahead of their time, fearless.

To say the business housed in 430 King's Road was run on unconventional lines was to put it mildly. Sometimes the shop would not open till early in the evening then would close after a couple of hours, the staff going off to The Man In The Moon or strolling a bit further down the King's Road to a Courage pub called The Roebuck.

McLaren talked to *Swindle* magazine about the background to the shop's switch: 'Having an independent store gave us the ability to create fashion in our own homes. Bernie Rhodes used to silkscreen all my T-shirts in his bedroom. Vivienne would be sewing them all up in our bedroom. Three or four out-workers would be knitting jumpers in their bedrooms. It was a total cottage industry.'

Westwood was not in the shop much at the start of 1974. She was working at home in her bedroom on her art. McLaren had also been taken by the ideas of Andy Warhol. Only now after his death can McLaren be ranked with Warhol as an artist – no, make that 'figure' – who made a difference.

One of the reasons McLaren had quit Goldsmiths College was that he had attended an exhibition of Andy Warhol's work which had revolutionised his thinking about modern art. Warhol had transformed the media to promote his image, and McLaren had this idea about running 430 King's Road like a smaller version of Warhol's Factory, a meeting place for quirky, inventive personalities. Warhol would have been flattered.

McLaren had recently read the book *SCUM*, by Valerie Solanas, who had shot and almost fatally wounded Warhol. He described her book as one 'of the most intense manifestos I had ever read. She seemed really crazy and I was inspired by her.'

Westwood made a T-shirt using some quotes from the book printed in blue and black on a white shirt.

One of her most famous creations was the 'Rock' T-shirt with leather armholes, a copy of a shirt made famous by Alice Cooper in the early '70s. At the time, Cooper toured with a French guillotine contraption and would stage nightly mock executions. Westwood had attached chicken bones to the shirt with small chains. These garments are extremely rare and regarded as priceless today.

The 'Vive Le Rock' T-shirts were always big sellers. McLaren and Westwood had made the T-shirts for the Bill Haley/Jerry Lee Lewis/Little Richard rock'n'roll concert at Wembley in 1972, but had overestimated demand. A high-street fashion shop later used the 'Vive Le Rock' logo, and Westwood herself adapted it by putting Little Richard's image on a muslin shirt and jiving it up with some Situationist jargon about a 'Punk Rock Disco'.

The muslin shirts went well, especially the 'Destroy' version with a huge swastika emblem on the front. It came with McLaren's stock reply to outraged passers-by: 'We are here to positively confront people with their past.'

Another of the most controversial items was the 'Cambridge Rapist' T-shirt with the leather hood image. The police were alerted and thought that the actual rapist might have been one of Westwood's punters. With McLaren away in 'the valley of the Dolls', the T-shirt was withdrawn as a result of police pressure. Upon his return from America, he was furious about the ban and quickly brought out another version. This incorporated a picture of Brian Epstein, the late Beatles manager, with the words 'It's Been A Hard Day's Night'. McLaren vented his spleen on the memory of Epstein by writing a few words about the manner of his death. It was all done to provoke. History, said McLaren, was 'for being pissed on'.

In 2008, Damien Hirst spent some of the cash derived from his lucrative visceral shock tactics, splashing out £80,000 on McLaren/Westwood punk clothing. Hirst intended to exhibit the pieces which would increase their value. Cash from Chaos. The problem for the unsuspecting Hirst was that the gear was not kosher, as no less an authority than McLaren himself identified them as counterfeits, as dodgy as the 'Tommy Fullfigures' in Surrey Street market. What a shower of phoneys. McLaren must have creased up. He told *The New York Times*: 'I felt terrible but they were fakes. Seeing these clothes I said, "Wow, they have gone to great lengths to manufacture the labels and distress the fabrics." But clearly they were not the fabrics we used 35 years ago, and the stitching was totally different.'

It's all in the stitching, and McLaren would know. He must have stitched more people than a one-armed surgeon in a Glasgow A&E on a Saturday night. Another thing that gave it away was the quantity, not only the quality. McLaren went on to explain: 'There were bags and bags, big black bags of them. We simply did not make that many. I mean, we literally made these clothes on my kitchen floor. They were each unique.'

The whole thing would have made a brilliant *Minder* episode. Arthur gets the chance to buy some vintage punk gear, Terry is not so sure about it. Toyah Willcox is the dodgy punk, bit part for Ian Dury, writes itself...

Westwood was rapidly becoming the most famous designer of the day, and perhaps the most famous of her creations was the bondage trousers. The idea of putting chains or straps between the legs of teenage girls turned the fashion world upside down.

Linder Sterling, singer with Ludus, grew up in Wigan before moving to Manchester. In 1974 she was studying art at the poly. She described to Simon Reynolds, in *Totally Wired*, the effect of the new clothing: 'I had been into the whole look of huge red stilettos and quaffs, all that second-hand American clothing. Which was still very brave in the North of England. But then, when you suddenly went punk! The first time I ever wore bondage trousers in Manchester, people did just stop in the street in a really ugly way. It was particularly scary for women.

'Never underestimate the power of the first pair of those trousers that Vivienne Westwood made – it was beautifully crafted and subtly subversive. There was continual abuse, from all ranges and both sexes. And lots of people I know were victims of really horrendous physical violence. I was beaten up.'

Go forward to 1993 and Duran Duran are on a comeback tour in America, riding on the crest of a wave with a hit single, 'Ordinary World'. Their photogenic keyboard player Nick Rhodes is on his way to a signing session at Tower Records on Third Avenue. Nick is looking slick, his hair dyed platinum-lilac. He is dressed in a scarlet satin jacket and – guess what? – a pair of Westwood's best bondage strides.

McLaren knew that fashion is all the more fascinating for being taboo, all the more seductive for being secret. The changing attitudes to sexuality and gender which started in the '60s were the key to this.

There is a direct link between Westwood's T-shirts and the work of Tracey Emin, particularly the Turner Prize-winner's famous embroidered textiles, square montages of fabrics with their witty slogans. Emin's work was entirely autobiographical: she could easily have been playing bass in The Slits in the '70s. She put down the reason for her amazing success as being that the 'psyche of the nation' was right for her. As surely as that psyche was ready in the '70s for Westwood.

McLaren loved the whole deconstructive nature of Westwood's clothes: 'The idea of a torn T-shirt thrown into a bucket of grey dye to make it look like an oil rag discarded by a mechanic.' It made it almost impossible to sell, and he liked the idea of having a shop where nothing was for sale.

'I like the contradictions of that; it turned our shop into a place people found impossible to leave.'

That was the vibe that McLaren wanted to put out. He thought a lot about the 2i's coffee bar in Soho and that was the atmosphere that he wanted to recreate. That is what attracted rough boys like Steve Jones to hang out in the shop with his chums. 'Mal's place was cool,' the Pistols guitarist said, 'cos you could hang out in there, with the jukebox and the sofa. We used to sit in there and watch people come in.

'After a while I used to hang out with McLaren. He used to go to the Speakeasy. I used to go down there on a Friday and wait for him to go down there because I could not get in. I was only 17 or 18 or so. I started driving him around to all these little tailors down in the East End because he could not drive.'

In fact, throughout his life McLaren made no attempt to drive.

Jones used to drive Westwood's Mini, its back seat always covered in patterns and materials.

Exactly why McLaren showed any interest in Steve Jones was open to conjecture. He remained McLaren's favourite Pistol right up until the end, and Jones had some kind words for his old boss. Conversationally blunt, tough yet affable, a handy lad, Stevie J. But underneath his loutish demeanour and yobbish behaviour was hidden a very sharp mind. To some extent, Jones acted as McLaren's 'minder' in tougher times. As his notoriety spread, this would prove to be of increasing use to him.

Steve Jones had been brought up on the tumultuous Goldhawk Road in Shepherd's Bush. In those days, before it became gentrified with TV and media people, it was one of the toughest areas in London. The High Numbers, before they metamorphosed into The Who, played at the Goldhawk Club in their early days. Pete Meaden would have been around then.

Lead singer Roger Daltrey always put it about that he was a product of that environment, although the truth was he had a nice middle-class upbringing in the Bedford Park area, in nearby Chiswick.

Jones was the real deal, and perhaps deep down McLaren was genuinely frightened of the characters he had created in Jones and Lydon. Frankenstein's monster put together by vampires.

Like McLaren, Jones had had a difficult childhood. He had a good relationship with his mother but he did not get on with his stepfather. Poorly educated, the only future open to him appeared to be petty crime.

Jones started to go down to the shop when it was Let It Rock, posing as a potential customer while his confederates helped themselves to any loose stock. Day-glo socks, belts, a few creepers, anything they could scavenge.

In those days he was trying to get a band together with a guy called Warwick (Wally) Nightingale, who had grown up in the same area as him and drummer Paul Cook. Already in trouble with the police, Jones was saved by Malcolm McLaren and music.

Paul Cook was the drummer in the band, originally called The Strand, after the song 'Do The Strand' from Roxy Music's second album, *For Your Pleasure*. Their first album was one of the most important records of the 20th century, as it set the blueprint for the revolt in style that followed it. As with the Pistols, the critics would review the audiences of their shows.

The artwork on *For Your Pleasure* was brilliant, featuring lingerie model Kari-Ann, with photography by Karl Stoecker, and crediting stylist Anthony Price for clothes and make up. The concept was by lead singer Bryan Ferry, once described by style expert Peter York as 'the best possible example of the ultimate art-directed existence'. In those days, Ferry lived in Kensington and McLaren would often see him walking down the King's Road to have his hair cut by Keith in the nearby Style Salon. McLaren was later to work with Roxy's producer Chris Thomas.

Ferry had his suits made by Tommy Roberts in his new boutique, Mr Freedom, where Bowie also shopped. Wally Nightingale alleged that he robbed Roberts of all of his stock, slaughtered him. When The Strand singer told McLaren, he shook his head in disbelief.

All Nightingale was interested in was taking Mandrax and drinking; McLaren knew that he was a tearaway and an accident waiting to happen. You could have a singer acting like a tearaway but not a tearaway acting as a singer. He knew that if the group was to make to make it they would have to ditch Wally, and he didn't look right anyway.

They played their one and only gig with him on vocals in Tom Salter's Café. It was in a room over the café, next door to the Birds Nest pub opposite the fire station, a really famous part of the King's Road in the early '70s. The Birds Nest was a disco pub called the Six Bells, run by an Irish guy called Dick. The music was immaculate, a lot of soul, Bowie and Roxy, and the Chelsea players used to drink in there on a Sunday night, in the days they mixed with the fans.

Salter's Café later became Pucci Pizza. In the closing

years of his life, George Best used to live in nearby Oakley Street, a few doors down from where Bowie had lived around the time McLaren was opening his first shop. Best's local was a tiny pub called The Phene tucked away between the Thames and the King's Road. The pub became his refuge for days at a time. Sometimes he would venture out to Pucci's to nibble on a pizza. Food was never a concern, though, to George, slowly drinking himself to death.

If he had been in the café that night, Best would not have heard much from The Strand; desperately unprepared, they did not have any songs. McLaren was still in New York but Westwood was there keeping tabs. She kept on moaning to the group, 'Get up and play.'

Eventually, the band jammed, some dirge based on Small Faces songs. Westwood was disgusted by the whole thing and sat with her arms folded, muttering about how bad it all was.

The other member of the band playing that night was Glen Matlock. Jones and Cook met him when he was working in the shop as a Saturday boy. Matlock never really got on great with Westwood when he worked for her, as he explained on the *England's Dreaming* tape: 'Was she all right? Well, she was and she wasn't. I always found her a bit unnecessary, a bit too intense. On top of that, they [McLaren and Westwood] were always, "We're on a mission," and all that. I just thought that it

Jordan outside SEX and *inset* a World's End label.

With Pistols drummer Paul Cook. © *Rex Features*

Above: The Sex Pistols at EMI in December 1976. © *Getty Images*

Below: Siouxsie Sioux (second left) and (far right) McLaren. © *Rex Features*

Above: The New York Dolls – McLaren's practice run for The Pistols. Left to right: Johnny Thunder, David Johanssen, Jerry Nolan and Sylvain Sylvain.

Below: The Pistols sign with A&M outside Buckingham Palace in 1977.

© *Getty Images*

Above: McLaren was arrested after the boat trip to promote 'God Save the Queen'.

Below: The infamous Sex Pistols interview.

The Sex Pistols live and *inset* Bill Grundy
leaves the office after the enquiry into his
interview with them. © *Getty Images*

Jones reads all about it. *Inset*: Artwork for
'God Save The Queen'.   © *Rex Features*

was a decent Saturday job, with decent money – although I could see their side of it. Obviously it was their thing, and I was part of it. I think they were both into it.

'She became a bit overbearing, you know. I have seen her since and we have got on fine. Except one Christmas, she introduced me to some people she was with, and she was like, "Oh this is Glen, used to be my Saturday lad." Pulling rank, you know. And she is very Thatcherite in a way.'

Glen Matlock was the most musical of the Pistols, the hub of the band. After he left, the Pistols only wrote four more songs – none of them of any merit. He was born on the Harrow Road and educated at St Clements Dane School, next door to Wormwood Scrubs. It was a grammar school and they wore a green blazer with yellow trimming.

Steve Jones also met Matlock when they played against each other in a five-a-side contest. Matlock obtained his job in the shop when he went in to buy a pair of creepers. Someone was leaving and he got the gig at £7 a day. McLaren had interviewed Matlock for the job, and the youngster found him rather aloof and sullen at first. Jones was a hooligan, the 'ruffian on the stairs' as Joe Orton once wrote, while Matlock looked too 'straight' (his term). McLaren opened up to him after he had been there a while, but there was always a distance between them, a faint tension. Bernie Rhodes, a frequent visitor, was more interesting, especially when he found out that the Saturday boy was an art student. Soon Rhodes was giving Matlock his own unique perspective on the complex subject of French Situationism, Dadaism and anything else that came into his head.

Matlock joined the shop when it was still called Let It Rock. He found the Teds no trouble at that time but most of them were really straight and dull. They could be divided into two types. The first was the older, hardcore Ted. These were the Edwardians with the half-moon jacket pockets and the huge creepers. Still trapped in another time, waiting for Eddie Cochran and Buddy Holly to make their comebacks. Westwood's Zoot suits attracted another type of Ted, younger, more fashionable, The Everly Brothers as opposed to Gene Vincent. The chaps – Jones, Cook, Nightingale – called them 'Showaddywaddy' Teds after the retro rock'n'roll group that had a string of hits in the '70s.

The summer of 1975 found Glen working through the holidays in the shop. He made the pink SEX sign and put it up, but nobody had any idea what was going to happen next.

CHAPTER SIX

THE NEW YORK DOLLS

'During Thatcherism if you did not fit in with the crowd you
were on the outside, and if you were on the outside you
were nobody. And that was the general feeling for
everything, no matter what your place was in the hierarchy
you had to fucking fit in, and, if you didn't, forget it.'

TRACEY EMIN

'We attract only degenerates to our concerts.'

DAVID JOHANSEN, NEW YORK DOLLS

In his splendid biography of Oscar Wilde, Richard
Ellman wrote about Oscar and his young wife
Constance strolling through Chelsea to visit a friend, the
artist Louise Jopling. Wilde described it in this manner:
'As we came along the King's Road, a number of rude
little boys surrounded and followed us. One boy, after
staring at us said: "Hamlet and Ophelia out for a walk.
I suppose!"

'I replied: My little fellow you are quite right.'

Oscar and Constance were the Posh and Becks of the 19th century, a fine-looking couple who made news wherever they went. Malcolm McLaren and Vivienne Westwood were the punk Posh and Becks, though a comparison to Bonnie and Clyde might have been more accurate, the Barrow Gang of West London. In reality, they were nearer to other Chelsea faces – Ashley and Cheryl Cole, the golden couple whose love was extinguished in the paparazzi flashes.

Ellman described Wilde as wearing a brown suit covered in buttons; Constance wore a huge white hat with feathers. Let us contrast this to McLaren strutting down the King's Road in his blue Elvis suit and Westwood in her bondage trousers. Style was everything to them, but they had created the clothes, while Victoria, Cheryl et al just wore them. Westwood was Ungaro's bird of paradise, McLaren a cross between Beau Brummell and JT Barnum.

When McLaren flew to New York to link up with The New York Dolls, it coincided with some shop business. An Englishman in New York, he travelled light. It was a good time for him, at last free from the tyranny of his grandmother. For years while at art school, New York was a distant lodestar, but now it was a welcome bolt-hole from London.

EB White had written: 'No one should come to live in

New York unless he is willing to be lucky'; Clint Eastwood once asked a punk if he was 'feeling lucky'. McLaren was not feeling particularly lucky because his relationship with Westwood was falling apart and he needed to put some distance between them. There were two main conflicts. Westwood had seen the potential of the business and wanted to expand it into the world-famous brand it later became. While he was in New York, Westwood's work was getting more and more recognition. However, McLaren had proudly boasted that, as soon as a shop of his started to make a profit, he would close it down.

There was also the 'usual husband and wife stuff', as Ashley Judd once spoke about Val Kilmer to De Niro in *Heat*. Although she was not physically beautiful, Westwood was very alluring. Singer-songwriter Tim Buckley, who visited the shop before his untimely death, thought she was 'heavenly looking'. He was most impressed with the lavender eyeliner that she wore all the time.

The New York Dolls were big on eyeliner and mascara. They became the most star-crossed band in pop history. The problem was, however, that people were just not ready for them at the time. They should have been the most indelibly famous rock stars of their generation. McLaren was attracted to the band because of their androgynous image and also the fact that, when he heard their debut album in September 1973, 'I thought it was the worst record I had ever heard, what mattered was that they were so good at being bad.'

Visually, the Dolls were a cross between The Rolling Stones and the English glam-rock band Sweet. Lead singer David Johansen was a Mick Jagger wannabe and the guitarist Johnny Thunders was a heroin addict. Thunders had dark hair cut like Ronnie Spector, lead singer of The Ronettes and one-time wife of their producer Phil.

The term 'Dolls' was interesting. Most people thought that it had a sexual connotation, but actually it was a drug reference. 'Dolls' were pills: barbiturates, uppers and downers, the 200 blues in the inside pocket of Pete Meaden's tonik jacket. The late novelist Jacqueline Susann exquisitely wrote a book called *The Valley Of The Dolls*; at one time, it was the biggest-selling novel on the planet, shifting 30 million copies. It was made into a cult film starring Sharon Tate, Roman Polanski's wife, who was slaughtered by Charles Manson's 'Family' shortly afterwards.

In 1972, the Dolls flew to England to open for Rod Stewart and The Faces at Wembley. McLaren's fledgling band members, Wally Nightingale and Steve Jones, had been at the gig, having kicked down a door to gain entrance. The Dolls looked outrageous with awful vaudeville flourishes, Nightingale remembered. The chaps rounded off the evening by gatecrashing Rod Stewart's backstage party and swilling down his Laurent-Perrier pink champagne.

That is the period when the Dolls visited McLaren's shop to try to score some clothes. They had first met in 1971 when guitarist Sylvain Sylvain, McLaren and Westwood all attended a New York clothing trade show. Sylvain had his own knitwear company called Truth And Soul. McLaren reminded the Dolls' musician of Jerry Lee Lewis with his long sideburns and drape jacket (Sylvain had never heard of Showaddywaddy).

The Dolls had a gig that night and McLaren and Westwood schlepped down to a Lower East Side club to check them out. The couple were impressed by the hard rocking of the prettified bunch and invited them to the King's Road next time that they hit London. That was how it got started.

The 1972 tour ended in tragedy when Gothic-faced drummer Billy Murcia died in his bath from a lethal combination of Mandrax and drink. Some said it was heroin, others said he just drowned. The title of the band's second album, *Too Much Too Soon*, would have been a suitable epitaph.

The Dolls came back the next year and McLaren and Westwood started following them about from show to show as the Dolls progressed into the realm of self-parody. It was Lurex tights, high heels and more makeup than Lily Savage. Johansen spent most of the show lasciviously licking the mike. The couple were present at Biba's Rainbow Room in Kensington and met *NME* writer Nick Kent there. Kent was on the fringes of McLaren's world, with aspirations to be a pop star, and had actually played with The Strand. Kent was a brilliant writer but with little discernible musical talent. To paraphrase Oscar Wilde, and quote another of his maxims, 'Those that cannot do it, teach it.'

Nick ranted about the show in the Mark Paytress book *The Art Of Dying Young*: 'The New York Dolls were kinda effete. The music was raw, but there was a limp-wristedness about what they did; it was still glam rock. The Sex Pistols could never flirt with sexual ambiguity. But the other ingredients were there for them to pick up on.'

When the Dolls played a gig in France at the Paris Olympia, super fan McLaren was in the audience somewhere. They did not go on stage till 3.30pm; Johnny Thunders threw up on it, his scarecrow body heaving, and Johansen's vocals sounded like the weird voices associated with transsexuals in the middle of hormone treatment. They were a putrid shambles.

Also in the audience that night was Nico of the legendary Velvet Underground, part of Andy Warhol's original circus. Nico was hiding out in Paris after glassing the girlfriend of the guy who ran the Black Panthers in New York.

The Dolls' management team quit to handle a band called Kiss who were just beginning their sky rocket to fame. Without the Dolls there would have been no Kiss, who recycled their basic personalities, attitudes and songs from the best bits of the Dolls and then mixed it up with theatrics. They could not fail, unlike Johnny Thunders and his pals.

Back in New York, the group were in a bad way, drinking and drugging themselves nightly. Thunders' drug problems escalated, while drummer Jerry Nolan contracted hepatitis from severe drinking as his self-destructive alcoholic energies raged.

When he got to New York, McLaren resided on 20th Street for the duration of his stay. The place was a dump but he loved it. McLaren had a pal on 22nd Street who ran a retro clothing store that was supplying attire and equipment for 430 King's Road. After meeting Sylvain outside the Chelsea Hotel, he learned of the band's dire situation. McLaren used his connections to get the Dolls a loft on 23rd Street recently vacated by a black group called Mandrill, who had broken up. It even had studio facilities.

Sylvain talked to Jon Savage about the difficulties the group faced: 'The significance of things is what is important, and that is why we never made it in America. We were popular, but we never really got accepted to the point where people would buy the records and keep you going to the next stage.

'We were always the rebels, the drag queens, all the rest of it, the band America did not know what to do with. That turned on McLaren even more. He always liked the rebels, the underdog.'

McLaren unleashed the first offensive of his cultural terrorism in America by creating the Red Patent Leather show. The gimmick was to dress the band in red vinyl to annoy the authorities and let them know that they were communists. Feelings about the colour red still ran high in America. The Vietnam War had torn the country apart and the 'C' word was a bone of contention to many. The band even had a song called 'Red Patent Leather' to validate their new dress code and political stance.

The next gimmick was to put up a huge Soviet flag with the hammer and sickle on stage to compound the outrage and convince the world that they were Commie-pinkos. The crazy flag stunt brought McLaren and David Johansen close for the first time. At the best of times they hardly spoke. David was very wary of McLaren's motives and this was about the only time they worked on a constructive project together. Needless to say, the tactics brought a storm of protest which effectively ended the Dolls' career in their homeland.

In Manchester, all this was being logged by a young Steven Patrick Morrissey, president of the UK branch of The New York Dolls' fan club. The man later to become the front man and singer with The Smiths finally tracked down David Johansen in the '90s and talked to Jaan Uhelszki of *MOJO* about it. 'He seemed weary of talking about that time and those two albums. And of course, because I had all these questions burning inside of me for the past 40 years, they all just splurged out. He kept saying, "Well, it was so long ago."

'David certainly changed my life though, Johnny Thunders did as well, but David was the one for me because he was so witty, really taking control of everything and had a complete disregard for the American music industry.'

The man who had a complete disregard for the English music business, Malcolm McLaren, just did not have enough time to turn things around for the Dolls. He was blamed for hastening the end of the band but they were on a collision course in any event.

McLaren spoke to Legs McNeil and Gillian McCain, the authors of *Please Kill Me – The Uncensored Oral History Of Punk*: 'It was my raison d'etre to be in New York. I ran away from London, I was just bored. The New York Dolls were an adventure I wanted to have.

'I tried to throw politics into the mill. There was the whole notion of the politics of boredom, and this whole idea of dressing the Dolls up in red vinyl and throwing them Mao's Little Red Book. I just loved messing with that kind of pop-trash culture of Warhol that was so catholic, and so boring, and so pretentiously American, where everything had to be a product, everything had to be disposable. I thought, I am gonna try and make the Dolls totally the opposite. I am not going to make them disposable. I am going to give them a serious political point.' McLaren had written a manifesto, 'Better Red Than Dead', to substantiate his actions.

After one show journalist Lisa Robinson asked Johnny Thunders, 'Are you a communist?'

Thunders's answer was simple and to the point: 'Yeah, do you want to make anything of it?'

The war in Vietnam had finally ended with the Americans having to pull out of Saigon; a lot of South-East Asia was turning red. The Watergate scandal was about to explode and bring down the presidency of Richard Nixon. As a young candidate Nixon had launched a fiery red-baiting campaign for a seat in Congress. He would have not approved of the soviet iconography worn by the Dolls.

When Nixon was being kicked out of the White House, Henry Kissinger said to him, 'History will treat you kindly.'

Nixon responded, 'That depends on who writes the history.'

The future singer of the Pistols was fond of using the quote 'History is written by the victors'. There were no victors, however, in The New York Dolls story, they could truly be called 'flamboyant failures', though, perhaps the most flamboyant of all the many failures that littered the history of rock music.

They broke up in Miami in May 1975, in the middle of a sleazy club residency that McLaren had booked them into. Things had become tough for them in New York, and on the 'see them before they die' circuit they trod like hamsters on a wheel. There had been a backlash caused by their controversial new image and their credibility, hard won from the tough New York audiences, had been badly damaged. Now they treated them with a vacuous indifference.

McLaren had another angle in playing tough red-neck areas, where most of the audience were bombed on boilermakers. He figured that playing on their home ground was an easy gig; there was more chance of confrontation and hopefully publicity if they played in hostile trailer-trash environments. It was a ploy he was to use for the Pistols in the future.

Johnny Thunders could not function in Miami without his dealers and flew back to New York with a venomous glaze in his eyes. Jerry Nolan had a similar problem with drugs and was anxious to get out of Florida, too: there was a desperation and insecurity in him that inexorably led to his death. The relationship between Thunders and Johansen had also soured. McLaren could not halt the slide and the whole thing just fell apart. At the end everybody had gone home except McLaren and Sylvain. The Dolls guitarist asked McLaren if he wanted to visit New Orleans, so the two of them took off in a hired car, a silver Chevrolet sedan. For McLaren, it was an intoxicating time.

So began a friendship that lasted until the day McLaren died. They had a fine time in New Orleans, now sadly devastated by Hurricane Katrina. Sylvain took McLaren on a trip of woozy neo-existentialism. The day was spent frequenting the old record and clothes shops that Sylvain loved. In the evening the pair hit the low-rent Louisiana bars drinking beer and eating bowls of popcorn crawfish. Sylvain told McLaren about the wonderful black 12-string guitarists that influenced his playing: Leadbelly, Robert Pete Williams and Hogman Matthew Maxie.

Nothing ever went smoothly for McLaren, though. At the end of their trip, McLaren wanted Sylvain to drive them back to Florida but he had no proper licence. In the end McLaren had to coach The New York Doll through his test at the Motor Vehicle Department in New Orleans, just outside the French quarter.

McLaren was very anxious to bring the Dolls and their new image to England. They much preferred playing in front of the cool English kids than in the dangerous, homophobia-riddled atmosphere that they encountered in Middle America.

McLaren never had a formal contract with the Dolls,

and he only really announced he was the band's manager when he returned to the relative security of England. Money was never discussed. Likewise royalties. Really, he was more a consultant/adviser/stylist than an orthodox manager. It looked good on his CV, though, managing one of the all-time cult bands. They never made the money Kiss acquired, but as John McEnroe once said, 'The older they get, the better they get.'

McLaren had a lot to do with putting Dolls bass player Arthur 'Killer' Kane into rehab. Kane was a chronic alcoholic who fought it all his life; later on, he was badly beaten in a mugging and suffered severe brain damage. In 2004, he died of leukaemia.

Sylvain estimated that McLaren's maximum investment in the Dolls was around $800. McLaren was too shrewd to lose any of his own money in the deal. That is why he was such a good businessman; no one ever turned him over. Like David Bowie's association with Iggy Pop, McLaren's deal with the Dolls gave him instant kudos.

It was once estimated that Colonel Tom Parker, who managed Elvis Presley, personally earned nearly $100 million from him. The Colonel was a degenerate gambler and when he died in 1997 he left behind only $913,000 in savings bonds and memorabilia. At the time of his death, Parker was writing a book about Elvis called *How Much Does It Cost If It Is Free?* While in

New York, McLaren avidly read up on the King's manager and his bodacious business deals. He was particularly impressed by the deal that saw all the income from Elvis recordings being divided 50–50 from the first dollar.

For McLaren, every dollar, every pound was a prisoner. He would tease Jordan in the shop about her wages and try to convince the punk model that he had already paid her. Jordan stated, 'He was such a laugh; he used to work in the shop sometimes. He used to pretend he had given us our wages when he had not.' Westwood, she said, was a teacher and 'she never lost that attitude'.

Leee Black Childers worked with David Bowie, managed The Stooges and Johnny Thunders. He talked on the *England's Dreaming* tapes about McLaren's time with the Dolls: 'I remember him spouting a lot of strange communist stuff that did not interest or convince me. I was thinking, I don't know who this guy is, but I hope he has got a lot of money because he seems pretty much a jerk. But he was not jerky, because he managed to pull out before they robbed him of whatever money he did or did not have.'

McLaren was undeterred by his experiences with the Dolls; they had served their purpose as a dry run for the tactics he would soon employ with the Pistols.

He thought that he had found the missing part of the jigsaw when he came across the breathtakingly daredevil singer Richard Hell (real name Richard Meyers). The whole new-wave thing in New York was exploding and the Hell-boy was one of its pioneers. He had been in a band called The Neon Boys, then had progressed to Television, one of the most influential of the new-wave groups. He later wrote 'Blank Generation', an instant punk classic and a phrase that was to be one of the most widely used in the punk vocabulary.

McLaren talked about his own personal vision of Hell: 'I just thought Hell was incredible. Here was a guy all deconstructed, torn down, looking like he had just crawled out of a drain hole, covered in slime, looking like he had not slept or washed in years, looking like he did not care about you! He was this wonderful, bored, drained, scarred, dirty guy with a torn and ripped T-shirt. I do not think there was a safety pin there. This look, this image of this guy, this spiky hair, everything about it, there was no question I would take it back to London. I was going to imitate it and transform it into something more English.'

Hell had been playing at a venue in New York called The Little Hippodrome in March 1975, shortly before the Dolls turned it in. McLaren talked at length to Hell about his growing disenchantment with Television and his differences with band member Tom Verlaine. Like Cook and Jones of the Pistols, Hell and Verlaine had grown up together. Legend had it that they both ran away from reform school to seek luck in New York. McLaren tried to persuade Hell to jump ship and go to England and start up a band. Hell declined the chance and instead formed a band with Johnny Thunders called The Heartbreakers which, plagued with massive egos and drug problems, was never going to last. After a couple of years, they split and Richard joined up with Sire Records. The decision by Richard Hell not to form a band in England was a crushing blow to McLaren's plans, as he saw Hell as the identikit profile of what he was looking for. Instead, McLaren appropriated as much of the DNA of Hell as he could – the haircut, the clothes and the style.

McLaren was lucky to be in New York at that exciting time but finally decided to return home. Like Sir Walter Raleigh, he said. Gone was the cashmere jumper and casual trousers, replaced with a lot of leather. McLaren's hair was longer and there was a hint of Brooklyn in his speech. One cold dawn he arrived back in London, Sylvain's white Gibson Les Paul under his arm. McLaren hoped that the owner would be shortly playing in England, but he never did and Sylvain ended up driving a cab in New York City until the remnants of the band re-formed.

Meanwhile, McLaren's relationship with Westwood on a personal level had floundered and for a while he lived with Helen Wallington-Lloyd. She put him up in her flat in Bell Street, which McLaren typically started using as an office. On the wall of 430 King's Road, he hung two posters that he had brought back from his trip that advertised Television and Richard Hell. One advertised the 'Blank Generation' – Hell had begun playing the song with Television in 1975; the other one listed some songs, one of which was called 'Venus' (later recorded on Television's 1977 debut album *Marquee Moon*).

McLaren was determined to ride the new wave he had found in New York and stepped up his search for a singer. He was telling everyone that he was putting together a group that was going to be the hottest thing in London and shake up the whole business. Meanwhile, Wally Nightingale was peremptorily sacked from the band and consigned to the dustbin of history. He never really recovered and served time in the '80s for drug offences before dying prematurely in 1996.

CHAPTER SEVEN

THE YOUNG ASSASSINS

An undistinguishable world to men
The slaves unrespited of low pursuits
Living amid the same perpetual flow
Of trivial objects, melted and reduced
To one identify, by differences
That have no law, no meaning , and no end
WILLIAM WORDSWORTH, *THE PRELUDE, BOOK VII,*
RESIDENCE IN LONDON

'McLaren was Fagin, always the conman of the first order.
He would be out with the people, and then denouncing
them for fun in the press, and no one really cared.
I do not think anyone felt it was personal,
they realised it was part of the ploy.'
DEREK JARMAN, DIRECTOR OF *JUBILEE* (1978)

One of the many urban myths about the Pistols was that John Lydon walked in the SEX shop and was discovered. The truth was that he was spotted by Bernie Rhodes walking down the King's Road. Ironic that it was Rhodes who went on to manage the Pistols' greatest rivals The Clash but was instrumental in securing for them their biggest star.

Lydon had spiky, bright-green hair and was wearing a Pink Floyd T-shirt that he had customised in a manner that would have made Vivienne Westwood proud. He had scrawled 'I HATE' on the T-shirt and gouged out the eyes of the figure depicted on the shirt. Ripped and torn in a manner that Richard Hell would have approved of, it was held together with those safety pins that Ian Dury thought he had the patent on.

Lydon always claimed that the look had been created out of poverty. Exactly what he had against Pink Floyd was never really established. In those days, they were part of the rock establishment, but their founder member Syd Barrett was the most famous and tragic acid casualty of the '60s. Syd became a true legend with his unique version of English psychedelia and became a huge influence on bands like Blur. Syd's mental disintegration ended his once glittering career. It was said that Barrett used to call himself Sid Vicious long before the youth called John Ritchie/Simon Beverley adopted it.

Lydon was asked to audition for the job of lead singer in the Sex Pistols. Another myth concerned exactly where the audition took place. Most theories have it being held on the premises of 430 King's Road, whereas another school of thought suggested that it was conducted in the nearby Roebuck. The pub was typical of the '70s boozers, almost the old 'spit and sawdust' variety, the sort of place that John Thaw and Dennis Waterman would operate out of in *The Sweeney* TV show. It had a mixed clientele, long hairs, football-hooligan types when Chelsea were at home, even a few Chelsea Pensioners from the nearby hospital.

When asked if he could sing, John snapped back, 'What do you mean? What for? No, only out of tune – and anyway I play the violin.'

Great answer, it must have gone a long way to getting the job. Already the caustic wit and withering sarcasm he became known for was being used to maximum effect. McLaren always ensured that the jukebox in the shop was well stocked. In the early days of Let It Rock, it was choc-a-block with Eddie Cochran and Gene Vincent, while Dave Berry's 'Don't Give Me No Lip Child' was another favourite. It would have certainly included the Alice Cooper songs that John did in his audition: 'Eighteen' and 'School's Out'. He should really have done 'No More Mr Nice Guy'.

McLaren gave John a shower head to warble into. Tonight, Malcolm, I am going to be a guy whose best pal was a snake. Paul Cook was there and was amused at the sight of this little guy, with deathlike pallor, screaming at the top of his voice, jacket hanging off him, arms whirring. Lydon later admitted how nervous he had been at the time, perhaps that is where the spasmodic jumping, a sort of truncated pogo dance, came from. That was also the first time that the 'hunchback' posing was thrown into the mix.

McLaren later described him as 'a hunchback with a handkerchief on his head'. He must have seen something in him, though, because he gave him the job. It was a pivotal moment in the history of punk. It was a defining moment because such was the brilliance of McLaren's packaging that, if you said punk, you immediately thought Sex Pistols. Lydon signed a contract soon after in the office of lawyer Stephen Fisher, although he later admitted that he did not bother to read it properly.

Another terrific irony was that Sid Vicious could have been the original singer. He was a regular in the shop and Westwood was the first to spot his potential. He was tall, with a Dennis the Menace haircut. Sid's striking appearance and aggressive manner made him, in Westwood's view, a perfect choice for the role. Later on, McLaren would always claim that the real star of the group was Sid.

Sid's mother Anne Beverley, tormented by the death of her son, committed suicide in 1996, shortly before the Pistols re-formed. Ann always claimed that it was Sid who had been the first person to take Lydon down the King's Road, long before the punk thing had ever happened. The day that Bernie Rhodes spotted Lydon in the Pink Floyd T-shirt, Sid was working in Portobello

Road market. It transpired therefore that his friend was on his own. How would things have turned out if Sid had got the gig first time round and Lydon had gone back to his dilapidated squat?

That evening after Lydon had told him about the successful audition, Sid returned home very down. He confided in Anne that he had missed out on an opportunity he felt was rightfully his. At the end, when everything had imploded, Anne was always of the view that McLaren had used Sid to extract his revenge on Lydon. But that came later, much later.

A few nights later, the band members met up in The Roebuck to meet the new boy and have a few beers. It was cordial but no real sparks flew between them; offstage it never did. The first rehearsal with Lydon up front was convened at a room in deepest Rotherhithe, called the Dippy Frog. Only Rotten turned up and was furious, it was a dangerous area to venture into, especially if you had bright-green hair. Right from the start, there were problems and it was to get worse, far worse.

McLaren threw himself into promoting the band and worked incredibly hard. He was pleased with the acquisition of Lydon; it gave the band something extra – an 'x factor' if you like. In an interview with the *Independent*, he explained how the name had come about:

'It came about by the idea of a pistol, a pin-up, a young thing, a better-looking assassin – a sex pistol.'

'And to launch that idea' he elaborated, 'in the form of a band of kids who could be deduced as being bad was perfect, especially when I discovered those kids had the same anger as I did. The anger was simply about money, that the culture had become corporate. My philosophy was, Fuck you: we do not care if we can't play and don't have very good instruments, we are still doing it.'

The assassin image was always popular in the media, coupled with youth and innocence. Ole Gunnar Solskjaer was one of Manchester United's most successful strikers in the Premier League era; the Norwegian player won the Champions League for them in the dying seconds of the final with an amazing goal. He was regarded as a hit-man, an assassin, of a player. The fact that he was extremely good looking, with very youthful features, earned him the sobriquet 'The Baby-Faced Assassin'.

Sir Richard Attenborough had a long career in the movie business but was best known for a part he played early in his career, that of Pinkie, a psychologically misshapen killer in *Brighton Rock*.

That was the look, and McLaren wondered what it would be like if a true sociopath was added to the delicate balance of personalities in the group. He didn't have far to look. Terrible consequences followed in the months ahead when a further damaged, violent personality was introduced.

Lydon could hardly have been described as a pretty face or even a poster boy for the punk generation. Only Matlock could have been regarded as boy-band material, but his place in the line up was soon under threat when Lydon joined.

At the start, McLaren thought that the band would be a great toy for selling the shop's clothes, a clothes horses for Vivienne Westwood's creations. Following McLaren's return from New York, the shop had gone from strength to strength under the auspices of Westwood. Orders were coming in and the shop was receiving press attention.

The argument as to whether or not McLaren manufactured the Pistols and was the Svengali/puppet master raged until he died. Lydon bitterly disputed any such claims and would always tell McLaren, 'You did not create me – I am me, there is a difference.'

McLaren did put it all together, though, as cynically and methodically as The Monkees were assembled in the '60s or, if you prefer, as skilfully as Louis Walsh selected Ronan Keating to work with Steven Gately and the guy in *Corrie* to make Boyzone. McLaren's corporate plan for success was coming together, trying to do with the Pistols what he had failed to do in America with The New York Dolls. His original plan had been to incorporate the quirky Richard Hell into the band and inject some proto-punk art, but in Lydon he had found somebody just as eccentric and, in his own way, astonishing.

Nick Kent recalls that the first time McLaren told him about his new discovery was when the pair were shambling down Denmark Street. He turned to the journalist excitedly and said, 'We have found a singer; he is the best thing in the group. He looks like a spastic, and he has just written a song.'

The word spastic seems a bit harsh now but it wasn't an uncommon term in those days. Ian Dury, a 'spastic' crippled in childhood by polio, had been fleetingly considered for the job, McLaren thinking he would have been an excellent choice. With Lydon struggling at first to get to grips with his new role, McLaren was quick to explain to him how unrelentingly good Dury was. McLaren pointed out to him how the Blockheads' leader had been influenced by Gene Vincent's style and also how manipulating he was with an audience. Dury went to his grave annoyed at how McLaren and Lydon had aped his style yet never given him any credit for it.

McLaren was not afraid to take anything in his quest for success. Imitation, in his book, was the sincerest form of flattery. If Dury was annoyed, then Nick Kent was shortly to be even more so. Apart from his dabbling with the Pistols, Kent had nearly formed a band with the electric Chrissie Hynde. They had been an item for a while but split up. McLaren wanted to call the group Masters Of The Backside for some reason only known to him. Another idea he had was for Hynde to front a band as a boy, and it was to include the cross-dressing Sylvain from The New York Dolls. Once again, it failed to materialise.

Hynde was a real piece of work during her relationship with Kent and secured a brief tenure with the *NME* as a writer. Then she worked at 430 King's Road for a while. Nick Kent's view of McLaren changed dramatically. As the Pistols became more famous, their manager's mistrust of the music press grew. In a sense he wanted the Pistols to outgrow the press, go outside it. What did Norma Desmond say in *Sunset Boulevard* about being 'too big for the movies'?

The Pistols' first gig was at St Martins School of Art on Charing Cross Road on 5 November 1975, Firework Night in Britain, which commemorated the failure of Guy Fawkes to blow up the Houses of Parliament. The first anarchist, in the not too distant future another bunch of anarchists launched an amphibious assault on the place.

It was Glen Matlock who got them the gig rather than McLaren. The bassist was supposed to do a Fine Arts degree but on his first day he bowled into the bursar's office and booked his band to play their inaugural show. Then he quit to throw in his lot with McLaren and the chaps. School's out for ever, as John sang to the shower head.

A band called Bazooka Joe were headlining, their singer a mesmerising lad called Stuart Goddard. It was the first time that he had crossed the path of McLaren but soon the world was to come to know him in his alter ego of Adam Ant, emerging from the first wave of punk to become the biggest superstar of the early '80s. Bazooka Joe was the name of a brand of bubblegum available at that time.

The band said they would lend their equipment to the Pistols, but after taking one look at Lydon supping some Red Stripe from a can they changed their mind. As luck would have it, the Pistols' rehearsal room was virtually opposite in 6 Denmark Street. It was a two-storey building at the back of a bookshop which doubled as a rehearsal studio and a flat where Jones and Cook lived in somewhat reduced circumstances.

The band just had to move their equipment across the road and proceeded to play a small set for about 20 minutes, including 'Pretty Vacant' and 'Problems'. Then they pulled the plug. The show was a disaster, with Steve Jones using Sylvain Sylvain's white Les Paul, a 100-watt amp, and the room packed but with no proper stage. A fight broke out in the audience.

The next day, Goddard quit Bazooka Joe to form his own band; he had a Bowie-esque capacity for change. Already the Pistols were beginning to influence things.

McLaren had just one agenda now and that was breaking the band and getting as much publicity for them as possible. He started to work incredibly hard; at night he would take his group around the clubs so they would be noticed. No matter how late he was out, though, he would always be in his office at 9.30 the next morning phoning round.

The first real publicity the Pistols earned was in February 1976 when they played the famous Marquee club in Wardour Street, even though McLaren hated the '60s heritage and the inflated reputation of places like the Soho club. The show they put on was fantastic, with people comparing it to the night that Iggy Pop played at King's Cross. They were supporting Eddie and the Hot Rods but completely blew them away. McLaren hated the prevalent pub-rock scene and he went to extraordinary lengths to avoid booking the Pistols on to that circuit.

Some of the Hot Rods' equipment was smashed. McLaren was giving the group licence to do exactly what they wanted, and, taking full advantage, Lydon was on incredible form. The band were playing badly off-key when he walked into the audience and sat down. Jokingly he said, 'I have always wanted to watch this group play.'

Jordan, outrageously attired in a peony-pink ripped top, sat down with him. She did not merely enter a room, she exhilarated it. Some people were saying she was the fifth Sex Pistol. Then the chairs started flying everywhere. Eddie and the Hot Rods had scored a hit with a song called 'Do Anything You Wanna Do', but it was the Pistols who were doing just that.

Neil Spencer, the *NME* features editor, had been

invited down to cover the Hot Rods, the acceptable face of the new wave. The *NME* was the most powerful of the music papers in those times. A real arbiter of taste, McLaren believed that 90 per cent of the music fan's brain was composed of what the music papers (*NME*, *Melody Maker* and *Sounds*) wrote about the current scene. There was a huge gap between the tabloids and the music press then. Today you have all the pop news splashed around in the tabloids. Not that there is that much excitement in music now; just like in football, all the sparkle and soul of it was sucked out years ago. The tabloids just cover celebs and *X-Factor* people.

When Spencer got there, the doorman told him to get in quick as there was a riot going on. Spencer wrote that evening up brilliantly with the headline: 'Don't look over your shoulders but the Sex Pistols are coming'.

McLaren could not have written it better. In a way he did because Steve Jones was quoted in the article as saying, 'We are not into music, we are into chaos.'

It was McLaren-speak, inventing his own language as Anthony Burgess did for *A Clockwork Orange*. Before the show, he had rehearsed the band with bravura spiel and endless quotes. Now he was dressed in leather jeans and a dark military-type jacket, and under his arm he carried a leather case.

As his offensive increased in the coming months, McLaren would speak to the press before the shows, quoting from his manifesto, the usual anti-music, anti-fashion diatribes, smacking of Situationism and Joseph Goebbels, Hitler's spin doctor. In the closing days of the war with the Russians pouring into Germany from the East and the Allies from the West, Hitler had sent out a directive from his Berlin bunker: 'Attack. Attack. Attack.'

That is exactly what McLaren was doing in the late winter of '76, attacking on all fronts, using every trick at his disposal. That was a huge night for McLaren; he had struck a blow against the establishment in one of its heartlands. There was a feel to it all that was undeniable. Eddie and the Hot Rods were not even mentioned in Spencer's review.

McLaren was overflowing with ideas at that time. At the time of his death, one of the many tributes was entitled 'The man who invented everything'. He was the first manager in pop to truly understand the power of the media and how to control it, with a direct link right up to the present day's spin doctoring. Now there were some new kids on the block and they were going all out to show that they were the toughest. He told the *Independent*: 'I was trying to do with the Sex Pistols what I had failed at with The New York Dolls.

'I was taking the nuances of Richard Hell, the faggy pop side of the Dolls, the politics of boredom, and mashing it together to make a statement, maybe the final statement I would ever make. And piss off this rock'n'roll scene. I was not starting anything new. I was waiting my turn to make the statement I had been trying to make since I was 14.'

The following night, Andrew Logan held a party at Butlers Wharf, near Tower Bridge. Logan staged the glamorous Alternative Miss World Contest and was pretty well unshakeable. The Pistols were on stage playing in a slapdash manner when some more music press turned up. McLaren panicked, the enemy were at the door; he wanted to do something outrageous, to cause a scene. He turned to Jordan, even more ostentatious that night, and asked her to take her clothes off. She was at first reluctant, but after some frantic negotiations she agreed to take her top off but only if Lydon assisted. Self-consciously he did and another iconic picture was born, later becoming a poster. Even the Logan set, blasé and jaded about most things, were rattled by the Pistols. Jordan lost one of her Manolo Blahnik shoes in all the commotion.

McLaren had been putting around the fact that, because of all the controversy that followed the band around, they were banned from playing, but the truth was they were busy. The next major incident happened at the Nashville on 23 April 1976. The pub was situated on the corner of Cromwell Road, next to the District Line station of West Kensington, within walking distance of Earls Court. A pub had stood on that site for over 200 years and was a tough environment. McLaren hated the pub circuit but the band was attracting a hardcore following now and he had to keep them operational, at least for the duration of the summer.

The band had played there a few weeks earlier but it had been a poor evening, plagued by problems with the PA and Lydon's ill humour. The singer felt the others were still treating him as an outsider, and it was starting to get to him. His bandmates did not socialise with him or make any attempt to get along with him. Lydon could never be at his best with the Pistols because he was never treated well. Compare this to Bowie who was always treated as a star even when he was not one.

Years later, Lydon found out that McLaren had asked Cook, Jones and Matlock to restrict their time with him because of the 'strangeness' of his personality. Even Vivienne Westwood in her school-teacher mode would comment on how strange she found John, because he collected records.

Westwood was at the centre of events that night when a fight kicked off in the audience. How it started was never clear. Dressed entirely in black leather with her peroxide hair, she looked like a punk version of Myra Hindley. One version was that, after returning from the bar, she found a hippie-looking girl in her place. There was a confrontation and the girl's boyfriend – a typical long-haired, plaid-shirted pub rocker – tried to intervene.

At that time, the Pistols had a small coterie of fans and supporters following them around. Realising Westwood might have been in trouble, they jumped in and gave the long hair a beating. Soon his face was a bloody mess. Some of the regulars in the Nashville resented the intrusion of the punks and joined in. 'It's off,' said Steve Jones jumping from the stage into the melee below. Within minutes, a massive punch-up was in full swing.

The press wrote it up like a Millwall v Chelsea hooligan battle. The atmosphere was the same, the cultures almost identical. The code of the Chelsea fans in the hooligan days was that, if one of their members was in trouble, then the rest would jump in. It was the same among the Pistols' followers. McLaren knew exactly what to do to trigger them; he even joined in himself, a surprise to some of the audience who saw him as an intellectual or some sort of parental figure.

Just as the young Rolling Stones under the shrewd management of Andrew Loog Oldham had represented the counter-culture by virtue of their bad-boy image, McLaren was doing the same thing. Among the pictures of the fracas, Sid Vicious could be clearly seen trading punches with the best of them. How Sid had even gained admission was a source of mystery to many as he had been ejected from the Nashville the last time the Pistols had played there.

Another apocryphal version of the story had

Westwood out of her seat and dancing with Chrissie Hynde, who that evening looked like she was fighting a retinal migraine. It must be said that Westwood was not the greatest of dancers. It was a source of amusement to Glen Matlock to see Westwood jiving around in the shop in her bondage trousers when one of her favourite songs came on the jukebox. She particularly liked strutting her stuff to a record by the Geordie R&B group The Animals called 'It's My Life'.

That night, she kept bumping into people, which eventually led to an argument. It was not clear if the future dame and Ms Hynde were dancing around their handbags at the time.

What did emerge, though, was that the fight had been stoked to cause maximum effect by Malcolm McLaren. Draw your own conclusions.

CHAPTER EIGHT

THE KING MIDAS OF ANARCHY

'Tin Pan Alley, do not forget that about McLaren, he is a salesman. McLaren is like Laurence Harvey in Expresso Bongo and Larry Parnes, but also there is the artist and he is a very intelligent person. There was a lot of spiv about him. He was like out to rob you.'

ADAM ANT

In the months leading to the Sex Pistols signing for Richard Branson's Virgin label in the spring of 1977, several far-reaching events happened. The punk movement took on a life of its own, the Pistols became the most notorious group in pop history, and Malcolm McLaren's attack on the hegemony of the music business manifested itself in the most coherent manner.

In Lydon, McLaren had discovered the necessary agent of his iconoclasm and the perfect symbol of the times. The future was theirs, although they were writing a song to the contrary. Lydon was now called Johnny

Rotten, a nickname given to him by Jones because of the poor state of his teeth. To this day, the majority of the public think that *is* his name.

Lydon was like a character from the London-based novels of Martin Amis, soon to burst on the literary scene with his unique style of writing. Like McLaren and Lydon, his whole career was a series of controversies. Lydon could have stepped out of the pages of Amis's best novel *Success*, set in the Chelsea area, the hunchbacked street urchin with the seagull eyes.

The summer of 1976 was a memorable one, the warmest for years and never bettered, unfortunately, in recent ones. Each year subsequently, those people who remember it use 1976 as the yardstick. An incident in the early summer of '76 was, at the time, dismissed as just another senseless act of violence, part of the mounting tide. Coupled with another unpleasant episode at the same venue a few months later, it gave some portent for the future. Sid Vicious was involved in both incidents.

In June, Nick Kent was attacked by Vicious at the 100 Club in Oxford Street. It was one of the most famous clubs in London, situated in a basement near Tottenham Court Road. Shortly before he took off on his last flight, the famous big-band leader Glenn Miller played there. At that time, the club was popular with the American servicemen on leave in the capital. Later on it was to feature The Rolling Stones, and McLaren saw The Pretty Things there in the '60s.

That night, the Sex Pistols were playing, and Kent was present together with two executives from Island Records, the company that had recently signed Eddie and the Hot Rods. There was still an element of bad feeling between the groups stemming from the incident at the Marquee. Kent said that he saw Sid at the front of the club in a huddle with both Lydon and McLaren, and Vicious pointed over to Kent. McLaren had already told the *NME* writer that he was now 'the enemy'. Kent alleged that McLaren was nodding his head as if to say, 'Go on do it.'

Kent continued the story in a selection of his writings, *The Dark Stuff*, where he curiously referred to himself in the third person. 'Sid and the others became a leering Gestapo for Lydon's Top Cat persona. Fuelled on sulphate and acid, they were the big noise now. They knew "the truth" and anyone threatening the autonomy was needful of a lesson in intimidation.

'In June Sid was dispatched to give such a lesson to a journalist. Assisted by another psychopath accomplice, who held a knife some two inches, no more, from this music writer's face. Sid aimed five good scalp-lacerating hits with his rusty bike chain. Only once did he hit his mark, causing much bloodletting but little damage.'

Kent published a further book in 2010 and in it he

expanded on the story, this time claiming that McLaren hired thugs to threaten anyone who challenged his position as the 'Pygmalion of Punk'. Kent was keen to promote this image of McLaren strutting around like Tony Montana in *Scarface* with a couple of anthropoids in tow ready to do his bidding at a moment's notice.

Kent never really recovered fully from the attack; he had a nervous breakdown and lost interest in the punk scene. *NME* then signed up Tony Parsons and Julie Burchill, who had responded to an ad in the paper for 'hip young gunslingers'.

The same month, the Pistols played at the Lesser Free Trade Hall in Manchester, another gig that has passed into folklore. McLaren was keen to book them in Manchester because he had heard about Tony Wilson, who presented *So It Goes*, a music and culture show, on Granada TV, and was keen to cross swords with him. The previous bands that had played there included Pink Floyd and David Bowie. It had been very theatrical but the Pistols blew all that away. As the late John Peel so amusingly put it, 'It was a breath of foul air.'

Wilson was in the Lesser Free Trade Hall audience that night and was not sure what to expect. He had heard a tape McLaren had touted of their Nashville show but was undecided; it sounded like it was recorded in a bucket. The audience was only 40-strong but they included some names that were to go on and dominate the business in the coming years, having been inspired by the Pistols. It included a strikingly camp Steven Morrissey, members of the band Warsaw (named after a Bowie song, they went on to become Joy Division), Pete Shelley of Buzzcocks, Howard Devoto of Magazine (who promoted the gig) and Mick Hucknall of Simply Red.

Like so many of the kids described in this book, Hucknall had a difficult childhood in the backstreets of Manchester. Hucknall went on to become one of the biggest-selling artists of the '90s and enjoyed more success than anybody in the punk scene. A great singer, he did it with a style of music totally different from the Pistols, but he displayed a degree of McLaren's intuition in his dealings with record companies, including setting up his own record company selling direct to supermarkets and online.

Devoto had read Neil Spencer's Pistols review in the *NME* and drove down from Manchester to check them out at college gigs in High Wycombe and Welwyn Garden City, supporting Screaming Lord Sutch, the man behind the Monster Raving Loony Party.

There was a big argument involving McLaren and the Lord over equipment, but Sutch was impressed with Lydon, another madman like himself, bright and funny. McLaren liked Devoto and was amazed that he had heard of the Pistols in Manchester. When the student union at Devoto's college refused to book the Sex

Pistols, he hired the small hall above the larger Free Trade Hall for an implausible £25. It was to be worth every penny.

McLaren spent time before the gig out in the street trying to hustle tickets; like Colonel Tom Parker, he was at heart what the Americans call a 'carny', drumming up the audience to sell a show. McLaren had this strange dark suit on, made of tweedy material, that an old Jewish tailor called Sid Green used to make up for him. Always obsessed with clothes, he had a pattern book of original fabrics that he would carry about.

The *24 Hour Party People* movie – starring Steve (Alan Partridge) Coogan brilliantly playing the part of Tony Wilson – featured a scene about the concert, but the McLaren character was not built up as it should have been. Not much is recorded about what happened between the two of them. McLaren knew about Wilson's rising reputation. They both had a common need to hustle as opposed to more conventional methods, and Wilson, like McLaren, would assume as much importance as the groups he became associated with.

As soon as the Sex Pistols broke into the old Monkees B-side 'I'm Not Your Stepping Stone', Wilson could see and hear what all the fuss was about. A whole bunch of crunch. It was also the first time 'Anarchy in the UK' entered their set, a key moment in the whole thing, along with the boat trip.

The Sex Pistols came back again in July for another show. This time there were about 1000 people present, and Wilson booked the Pistols on *So It Goes* for their first TV performance. Wilson was years ahead in his thinking. Warming up with 'Problems', Matlock broke a string and sat on the stage putting on a new one. As the technicians and crew worried about the show over-running – because of the overtime rates and scheduling – Wilson took the opportunity to come over to Lydon and ask him why he had refused to do an interview earlier on.

''Cos you're a cunt,' was the ever-direct reply. The live audience of about 300 people watched as Wilson went bright red in embarrassment. Journalist and media commentator Clive James was on the show that night, too. Lydon seriously hated him, and would turn off the TV whenever James made an appearance, which at the time was often. The blustering James tried to take control of the situation and started throwing questions and instructions to Lydon.

The Sex Pistols vocalist exploded with rage and tore into the Aussie, destroyed him totally with a torrent of high-speed abuse. It was simultaneously highly amusing and yet terrifying, such anger, such contempt.

After their very quick appearance on the show they were packing their gear away and an old boy came up to Lydon. He thanked him for his outburst against James, telling the singer that it was the best thing he had seen on a TV show. McLaren was at the back of the studio, staring at Lydon with a mixture of admiration and detachment. Lydon thought that the Pistols had put on an awful performance.

Wilson would later name his influential Manchester club the Haçienda after Ivan Chtcheglov's declaration 'the haçienda must be built', part of the political theorist's idea of a utopian urbanism. Chtcheglov was a major inspiration to Situationist International, which Wilson had become interested in when he was at Cambridge. The college he attended was responsible for the translation of Debord's book *La Societe Du Spectacle* (*The Society of the Spectacle*), which McLaren quoted heavily from.

Wilson spoke of McLaren to Simon Reynolds in *Totally Wired*. 'Let us remember that punk was a massive mistake for McLaren. His idea was to create a Bay City Rollers of outrage. What he wanted was to have the biggest pop group in Britain just because it was revolting. Instead, his pop group was the biggest group in Britain because it was the most fantastic piece of art of that decade.

'McLaren – you don't want to believe a word he says. He is my greatest hero, but you would not want to believe a single word. History took over and what he created grew and grew.'

Great insight by the man who formed a record company just to release records by Joy Division. For the first time since he put the thing in motion, McLaren must have had the feeling that it was starting to run away from him. From the start he had pumped out the belief that the Pistols 'could not play'. Nothing could be further from the truth. The tight-knit combo of Cook and Jones had been playing together for a couple of years and had formed a fine understanding. Despite his limitations as a singer, Lydon was the most charismatic front man in rock. Matlock, despite his problems with Lydon, was the best musician in the band, who had mastered that jangly Rickenbacker/Byrds guitar sound and wrote the bulk of their songs. 'Anarchy in the UK' was a brilliant song. It was both highly focused and primal, each line creating an expectation for the next. McLaren just looked stunned when he heard it that night in Manchester. By the time Lydon started singing the list of armed political parties, he was totally blown away.

The cracks were starting to appear, however, and Vicious, not even in the group at that time, was to cause immense problems. Lydon once caustically remarked that 'he was better in the crowd than in the band'. Even in the crowd, however, he was a threat to their stability with a total defiance of taste and manners.

In September, they held the Punk Special or, as it

became more commonly known, the 'Punk Festival' in the 100 Club. It was the movement's Woodstock moment, featuring the biggest names of the era. McLaren put it all together with Bernie Rhodes, by now managing The Clash. They were on with the Pistols that first night. Also on the bill were the brand-new Siouxsie and the Banshees and the Subway Sect, two bands put together out of the followers of the Pistols. McLaren was expanding his empire; he wanted a roster of acts like Brian Epstein had in the '60s with The Beatles, Cilla Black, Billy J Kramer and others.

Kohl-eyed Sioux (born Susan Ballion) was a prominent member of the Bromley Contingent that formed the bulk of the Pistols following in the early days. She went on to become the first lady of punk and enjoyed a career that spanned four decades. If Vivienne Westwood was the Grande Dame of fashion, then surely Siouxsie was the Grande Dame of music. Always a keen follower of fashion, she discovered Let It Rock before she even learned about Lydon and the gang.

That night at the 100 Club, her voice was as flinty as ever. The gig had come about when McLaren announced that he had a vacant space for a group on his festival bill. He hated the '60s with a passion but was not afraid to borrow some of its better ideas. Another similar one was the old '50s/'60s package-tour idea with groups only playing short snappy sets about 15 minutes long and sharing gear. Working outside the established rock system, McLaren could micro-manage it all.

Siouxsie told McLaren she had a band available when the truth was she didn't. It was hurriedly formed overnight and turned out to be the equivalent of a punk 'super group'. It had Sid Vicious on drums, Siouxsie's long-term partner Steve Severin on bass and Marco Pirroni on guitar. Pirroni became very successful when he teamed up with ex-Bazooka Joe singer Stuart Goddard – Adam Ant.

Another huge '80s star, the relative unobjectionable Billy Idol, was pencilled in the line-up but pulled out because they would not let him do his own songs. Later Idol became huge in America, thanks to MTV. McLaren saw the potential in him but it never progressed to anything.

Siouxsie had made her name up the night before the gig and added the 'Banshee' tag from an old horror film. She thought it sounded great; McLaren just smiled and shook his head. They had no songs prepared, so the set was a glorified feedback jam that was loosely based on an old Velvet Underground song, 'Sister Ray'. Sid was tastefully dressed in a swastika T-shirt, the 'Belsen Babies' one. Vicious had a thing about Belsen: one of the few songs he wrote was called 'Belsen Was A Gas', another was 'Postcards From Auschwitz'. Sioux wore a conspicuous swastika armband and Pirroni had on one of Westwood's Anarchy shirts with Luftwaffe badges. They looked like extras from the Third Reich movie *The Damned*.

Sid tried to get into the spirit of it all, woefully doing his best Moe Tucker impression, but most of the audience were bemused by the whole thing. McLaren's statement about 'Not just being about the music' never sounded truer.

The Damned, the punk group named after the film, played the next night at the festival while McLaren was up North with the Pistols. There was a lot of rivalry and tension between the punk bands, McLaren adding to it by letting Lydon openly denounce rivals like The Clash in the music press. Sid hated The Damned; in fact, he hated any punk band other than McLaren's: they were as much an enemy to him as Nick Kent.

Sioux didn't like the band either and stood moaning about them to Severin. Sid said nothing, supping his pint, then suddenly he flung the glass at The Damned. He was as good a chucker of things as he was a drummer and the badly aimed glass hit a concrete pillar by the stage and exploded into hundreds of pieces. One of the pieces tragically took the eye out of a 17-year-old girl standing down the front.

The police quickly arrived on the scene and Vicious was led away by the plod. It is significant that a young policeman was on duty in the club in plain clothes, well punk chic. A real contradiction in terms on all levels. Already the authorities had the punk movement under surveillance. This pre-dates Spooks and all that stuff, but, once an unruly mob appears talking about revolution, anarchy and subversion, you can be pretty sure MI5 will take a keen interest. Today the names of everyone present at the festival would be on a database somewhere.

They must have been keeping tabs on McLaren since day one, since he organised the Croydon College sit-in with Jamie Reid in his art-school days, coming up on their radar as a potential subversive and troublemaker. The enemies of the state were no longer communist gentlemen (The New York Dolls?) but home-grown anarchists, socially adept and bright, also capable of handling all types of problems and personalities (Lydon, Jones and Vicious for a start). A peek at the file kept on Malcolm McLaren would be fascinating. Perhaps McLaren was a double agent; consider the irony, the counter-surveillance. *The Perfect Spy*, as John Le Carre wrote.

Vicious was sent to Ashford Remand Centre where he spent a week, good training for his future trip to Rikers. The story put about by his mother was that they gave him a hard time there. McLaren did not visit him, he had no real economic value to him at that time, but Vivienne Westwood did, the pre-gothic seamstress bringing him a book called *Helter Skelter*, about Charles Manson. The title came from a Beatles song his Family daubed on the walls of Sharon Tate's house, in her blood. Vicious found the book fascinating and it became a firm favourite with him. (He was finding Debord's *La Veritable Scission dans L'Internationale* hard going.) The phrase that struck Sid among all Manson's ravings was the bleak coda of nihilism: 'No sense makes sense'.

The following July, Sid appeared at Wells Street Magistrates Court on charges relating to the incident. He was found guilty and fined £125 for illegal possession of a flick knife (a favourite weapon of the Teddy Boys).

No charges were ever made against him for the loss of the young girl's eye. It was said at the time that the prosecution had not gathered enough evidence to press charges. This book is studded with the wisdom of Malcolm McLaren, the wit of Malcolm McLaren and the observations of Malcolm McLaren, but the following statement made to the *Independent* seemed very much out of context: 'The violence was magnificent. It was something that gave all those kids a terrific identity, made them proud of their future. So someone got blinded? Well, there are far worse things happening in places with far worse courses. One person blinded, a couple of people badly hurt – the achievement outweighed it completely.'

A crass thing to say, the blinding of the young girl was an awful event. She never came forward to explain her feelings or hurt over Vicious's callous act. Imagine that today? The media would have put her under such pressure and, of course, Sid would have been demonised.

Shanne Bradley, who later played in The Nipple Erectors with Shane MacGowan before he formed The Pogues, was a Pistols fan right from the early days at St Martins. She was in the crowd the night Sid chucked the glass and told Jon Savage, 'I was standing in front of the girl who got blinded. I was hardly aware of it at the time. Sid did throw the glass.

'John Lydon came up to me 'cos he could not believe how I was dressed. He asked me if I had ever been to the SEX shop. He said there was a girl called Jordan who dressed like me. He said I should go down there.

'I went down there with a friend. We got taken out to lunch by Malcolm McLaren. He took me round the shop and explained how all the clothes were made. There was a lot of rubber, very unusual. McLaren gave me his number and when I phoned him he said Vivienne Westwood was giving a talk at the ICA which I went to.

'A few weeks later I turned up at the 100 Club. McLaren was really offhand, didn't want to know me any more. He was very friendly at first. I could have got them a gig at St Albans but he said, "St Albans, no – not gonna do that. Waste of time."'

An interesting insight into McLaren's mutability. Bradley was one of the most striking figures on the punk scene. Yet another victim of a terrible childhood, she made herself look as hideous as possible to shock her teachers. McLaren must have seen something in her unique combination of waif-like charm and vulgarity that he could have used to promote either the shop or the Pistols. When he changed his mind for whatever reason, he saw no reason to continue being pleasant to her.

On 8 October 1976, the Pistols signed with EMI Records for an advance of £40,000 spread over two albums. Soon the house of McLaren was going to be filled with the sound of ringing cash registers. Polydor Records courted them strongly but McLaren was only interested in doing business with EMI. He considered them to be the epitome of the old music establishment and wanted to drive a stake through their heart. A chap called Nick Mobbs had finally persuaded the suits at EMI to take a chance with the Pistols. A few of the board members were still unconvinced and felt trouble was ahead. They were not far wrong

McLaren had also dealt with Dave Dee, the A&R man at Atlantic. Dee, a former policeman, had by a quirk of fate been on duty in the local police station where Eddie Cochran's guitar had been impounded following his fatal car crash and the policeman had taught himself to play on the instrument. He went on to have a string of hits in the '60s with Dave Dee, Dozy, Beaky, Mick & Tich, and bonded easily with McLaren, but the Pistols manager declined to take up his offer to sign the band for a 'single or EP and see what happens'. McLaren was holding out for the big bucks, a couple of albums and a wedge. He had a great turn of phrase, of describing mundane things as merely 'tea and cakes' if they were not important enough to him. Dee's offer was in that bracket, and he had no interest whatsoever. The Atlantic man was irritated by McLaren's attitude and was openly critical of the Pistols manager in the press, accusing him of being 'stupid and wanting the world'. Tony Montana wanted the world and everything in it.

McLaren stuck out for a deal and landed the biggie. Dee did not realise that McLaren had been playing him. Paul Cook would always praise McLaren for being the face of the band for the record companies.

Now the plan was to get a single out and quickly: McLaren still firmly believed that the punk scene only had a short life span and that the whole thing would soon melt away.

The Hollies, Manchester's finest group of the '60s, produced a slice of psychedelia with their 1967 single 'King Midas In Reverse', written by future Crosby, Stills & Nash superstar Graham Nash. Full of biblical allusions, it told of the protagonist's ability to turn things to dust rather than gold. In that short period,

McLaren was the King Midas in the song turning anarchy into gold. The money started to pour in as a result of his stunts, but soon it was to turn to dust.

It did not work out as smoothly as EMI hoped. McLaren wanted their own soundman Dave Goodman to record 'Anarchy in the UK' for their first single. It was recorded at the Wessex studios in Highbury, not far from McLaren's grandmother's old house. EMI sent down their best producer, Chris Thomas, who had worked on what was always known as The Beatles' *White Album* and Pink Floyd's *Dark Side of the Moon*, to cut the record. It was released on 26 November in a plain black sleeve. A few days before the chaps were supposed to go on TV to be interviewed by someone called Bill Grundy.

CHAPTER NINE

BILL GRUNDY

DATE: 1 DECEMBER 1976

Dramatis Personae: Left to right as the TV cameras would have picked them out. John Lydon, Steve Jones, Glen Matlock, Paul Cook. Bill Grundy, the *Today Show*'s feisty presenter, is sitting to the left of the screen. Behind the Pistols are the cream of the Bromley Contingent, Siouxsie Sioux (fresh from her success at the 100 Club), Steve Severin, Simon Barker and a young lady called 'Simone'.

This is a transcript of Bill Grundy's interview with the Sex Pistols on that day, broadcast by Thames Television.

GRUNDY [To the camera]: They are punk rockers. The new craze they tell me. Their heroes? Not the nice clean

Rolling Stones... you see they are as drunk as I am –
they are clean by comparison. They are a group called
the Sex Pistols...

JONES [Reading the autocue]: ...in action

GRUNDY: Just let us see the Sex Pistols in action.
(Come on kids)

*Live film of the Pistols is shown: looks like 'No Fun'
being played, possibly in the 100 Club.*

GRUNDY: I'm told that the group [hits knee with a
sheaf of papers] has received £40,000 from a record
company. Doesn't that seem, er, to be slightly opposed to
their anti-materialistic view of life?

MATLOCK: No, the more the merrier.

GRUNDY: Really?

MATLOCK: Oh yeah.

GRUNDY: Well, tell me more then.

JONES: We've fuckin' spent it, ain't we?

GRUNDY: I don't know, have you?

MATLOCK: Yeah, it's all gone.

GRUNDY: Really?

JONES: Down the boozer.

GRUNDY: Really? Good Lord! Now I want to know
one thing...

MATLOCK: What?

GRUNDY: Are you serious or are you just making me...
trying to make me laugh?

MATLOCK: No, it's all gone. Gone.

GRUNDY: Really?

MATLOCK: Yeah.

GRUNDY: No, but I mean about what you are doing.

MATLOCK: Oh, yeah.

GRUNDY: You are serious?

MATLOCK: Mmm.

GRUNDY: Beethoven, Mozart, Bach and Brahms have all died...

ROTTEN: They're all heroes of ours, ain't they?

GRUNDY: Really... what? What were you saying, sir?

ROTTEN: They're wonderful people.

GRUNDY: Are they?

ROTTEN: Oh yes! They really turn us on.

JONES: But they're dead!

GRUNDY: Well, suppose they turn other people on?

ROTTEN [under his breath]: That's just their tough shit.

GRUNDY: It's what?

ROTTEN: Nothing. A rude word. Next question.

GRUNDY: No, no, what was the rude word?

ROTTEN: Shit.

GRUNDY: Was it really? Good heavens, you frighten me to death.

ROTTEN: Oh all right, Siegfried...

GRUNDY [turning to those standing behind the band]: What about you girls behind?

MATLOCK: He's like yer dad, innee, this geezer?

GRUNDY: Are you, er...

MATLOCK: Or your granddad.

GRUNDY [to Sioux]: Are you worried, or are you just enjoying yourself?

SIOUX: Enjoying myself.

GRUNDY: Are you?

SIOUX: Yeah.

GRUNDY: Ah, that's what I thought you were doing.

SIOUX: I always wanted to meet you.

GRUNDY: Did you really?

SIOUX: Yeah.

GRUNDY: We'll meet afterwards, shall we? [Sioux does a camp pout]

JONES: You dirty sod. You dirty old man!

GRUNDY: Well, keep going, chief, keep going. Go on, you've got another five seconds. Say something outrageous.

JONES: You dirty bastard!

GRUNDY: Go on, again.

JONES: You dirty fucker. [laughter from the group]

GRUNDY: What a clever boy!

JONES: What a fucking rotter.

GRUNDY: Well, that's it for tonight. The other rocker, Eamon, and I'm saying nothing else about him, will be back tomorrow. I'll be seeing you soon. I hope I'm not seeing you [the band] again. From me, though, goodnight.

The signature tune plays and credits roll, Lydon looks at his watch, Jones starts dancing to the music.

McLaren wrote a little piece on the incident in the booklet that comes with the interview.

'EMI became my label of choice. It was English through and through.

'While rehearsals were under way for the forthcoming Anarchy in the UK tour, the EMI press department called excitedly. "Queen, the pop group, have cancelled the *Today* show, so we have got your band the spot instead! It's going to be a blinder! We're sending a car immediately." The band was not in a great mood. They never were. They hated each other. Over at the Thames TV station, we all gathered in the green room and drank ourselves stupid. Finally everyone was called into the studios.

'The record, "Anarchy In The UK", needed to create an eruption. After all, it was just a record and somehow that didn't seem to be enough. I refused to put a pretty picture of a band on a cover. Instead I instructed the marketing department to produce a plain black cover with no hole in the middle, no name, no title, no record label. Nothing. EMI were not happy. How, they asked, will anyone find the record?

'They didn't understand that I did not want just anybody to find it. I wanted only those who cared.

'The following day after the infamous interview on the *Today* show, Leslie Hill, the managing director of EMI, called my home. I had to be in Manchester Square in minutes. There had been a meeting with EMI's senior management, a statement needed to be issued to the press and they wanted me there. On my arrival, I was ushered into an office where Hill was pacing the room. The morning's papers were strewn across his desk. "What was I going to say?" he asked.

'"Simply boys will be boys," I replied.

'"Good. I think I might say that too."

'Perfect, I thought. The press are going to have a field day.'

'Boys will boys', the phrase McLaren always remembered from when his grandmother used it in front of the angry school authorities. It was strange but the incident that led to the biggest fallout in the history of punk rock was almost incidental and not some masterstroke from the puppet master. Or was it? McLaren rarely spoke about the actual Grundy interview. It was always strange that he did not appear before the cameras. Why wasn't he seated next to Steve Jones when he started his swearing act? McLaren was very shrewd. The next day it was open season on the Pistols. They were the No 1 targets for every boot boy, hooligan and vigilante in town. McLaren, furling his eyebrows at the whole thing, knew that, if he was sitting down the front with the Pistols, he would be drawing a big bull's eye on his face.

A few days after his father's death, Joe Corre wrote a tribute to McLaren in the *Observer*. He said that the best memories of his dad were chaotic but brilliant: 'I remember when, after the Sex Pistols swore on the Bill Grundy TV show, we were barricaded in our flat with the National Front trying to smash our windows.'

There was no record of McLaren ever mentioning such an event in his lifetime. Perhaps he kept it all low key to safeguard his family.

Analysing the interview again after all these years, a few things were very apparent.

Bill Grundy was, as he tells us early on in the interview, drunk or at least working on it, to the extent that he was not in control. He was 53 at the time of the show and strangely enough the first TV presenter to welcome The Beatles on to television, back in 1962 when he was working for Granada TV. The Pistols debacle effectively killed his career as he was immediately suspended and the show axed two months later. At that time, it was one of the most popular shows in the London region and went out live. Being an early-evening show, before the 9pm watershed, there was a strict code of behaviour imposed. The Christmas party season had started early and Grundy had started right along with it, enjoying a long lunch earlier that day with *Punch* magazine. What happened later would have graced the pages of their periodical.

Eric Hall, who later became a famous football agent (amongst his clients was Chelsea star Dennis Wise who, like the Pistols, was always in trouble), was then promotions manager for EMI. Queen was one of the bands he hustled for. They were enjoying a three-month spell at the top of the charts with their bombastic hit 'Bohemian Rhapsody', the complete opposite of what punk rock stood for. When Queen pulled out of the Grundy show, for reasons never really explained, Hall quickly arranged for the Pistols to step in. Hall had a catchphrase: 'Monster, monster'. He would be 'monster busy', but that evening there was 'monster trouble' brewing as the monster that McLaren had built in his King's Road lab started to run amok.

The transcript of the interview indicates that Steve Jones was the guy that did all the damage. The first problem arrives when he tells Grundy that the Pistols 'fuckin spent' EMI's money. Grundy appears to either mishear the swear word or chooses to ignore it, hoping that everybody else did. Perhaps he swore so much himself it just did not register.

Soon after, Grundy goes off on a tangent about Beethoven and Mozart before Rotten, as he was known, makes him lose the thread. Clearly, the researchers had tipped off Bill that if/when the trouble kicked off it would come from him, which is why he honed in on Lydon when he mumbled a very minor swear word under his breath. Lydon already seemed bored by the whole matter.

Enter Siouxsie Sioux, shamelessly milking every second. She described the evening to Jon Savage. 'I was blonde then, with one eye and a star, I was very pert and cheeky, very Larry Grayson. This horrible old man was trying to chat me up and I was going, "Well, really. Whoo!" Rather than fuck off, you dirty old man, get you.

'I got a feeling McLaren was geeing them up. Maybe stirring it a bit. The group were trying to act nonchalant, but probably a bit nervous as well. I vaguely remember McLaren sowing the seeds.'

Siouxsie looked amazing that night against the pallid, scruffy Pistols. Exotically dressed, like some punk dominatrix, she must have given a jolt to the slightly tipsy Grundy. Posterity has been kind to Sioux; that was the night it all started for her. It was a masterstroke of McLaren's to include her in the line-up. She was the catalyst along with Jones. Jones admitted that he was paralytic, that there had been six bottles of wine in the fridge in the hospitality room. Two of them had been guzzled by him alone. Jones always wanted the 'dirty bastard' soundbite made into a ring tone. Cash from Chaos. Matlock claimed that Grundy was in a bad mood because he had heard about the Pistols' troublesome reputation and did not want to interview them in the first place. The producer had pulled rank and Grundy took solace in the drink. The rest as they say was history.

Directly after the show, pandemonium broke out as the switchboard was jammed by irate callers. Siouxsie took it upon herself to answer some of them and began swearing back at the callers. Oh, what fun. Matlock was going back into the green room to have another drink when McLaren grabbed him and hustled him and the other Pistols into the Bentley. They just beat it out in time as a Black Maria arrived and half a dozen police piled out, presumably to arrest the foul-mouthed punks. It would have made the best *Carry On* ever. Kenneth Williams as the floor manager and Barbara Windsor as one of the Bromley girls.

Matlock claimed they went back to rehearsals for the 'Anarchy' tour, but Lydon told a slightly different version to *MOJO* magazine.

'McLaren panicked, the police being called. They had a rent-a-car outside. They drove off. They left me. They all went to Harrow or some party they had and dropped me off at Baker Street and I had to take the train home with no money. And look, I've just been insulting people on TV.'

Nobody was really prepared for the media reaction the next day. That's where *The Filth and the Fury* movie came from: some of the tabloid headlines were classics.

'Must We Fling This Filth At Our Pop Kids?'

'I Kicked In My TV Set Says Angry Father Of Four.'

The second one was some moron they set up, a lorry driver, obviously not used to swearing. There was a picture of him standing next to his smashed TV.

Things were never the same for anyone connected with the Grundy event. Jones perhaps put it best when he made the point that before Grundy-gate it had been about the music, but after the *Today* show it was just the media. The tabloids moved in and played on the lowest common denominator that they always impose on the working class. Malcolm McLaren had introduced the art-school sophisticated angle to punk rock. This had its basis in the Situationism doctrine that he had employed so cleverly; the 'throw off the shackles of oppression – change history' angle. That is why you had plain-clothes officers checking out things like the Punk Festival and McLaren's phone would have been tapped for sure. These guys were a genuine threat to society because they had a plan and could articulate it in a meaningful manner to the young.

Then, one tea time, the Pistols go on TV and start swearing. Immediately, the whole perception of punk changed – now it was about swearing and safety pins, strange-looking girls and leather jackets. It's Sid Vicious glassing people and hitting them with bicycle chains. Not about subversive songs about anarchy or trying to help yourself. The smart people like Sioux had seen the change coming even before Grundy downed his first glass of wine. The fashion was slowly changing. The Clash in Doc Martens and creepers was another sign of the direction it was headed. When Sid was nicked at the 100 Club, he was wearing orange jelly shoes. McLaren was still wearing his famous grey-black crepe-soled brothel creepers.

The night the Grundy show went out, Johnny Thunders and The Heartbreakers flew in to London, bringing with them biker jackets, a groupie called Nancy Spungen and heroin. The scene was changing literally overnight, and that night was 1 December 1976.

The papers made it into a national scandal. It's hard to think of anything comparable these days – possibly if Katie Price/Peter Andre or Cheryl/Ashley Cole had entered into some bizarre suicide pact. The Pistols were now tabloid famous – Cheryl Cole famous. No, make that Jack Tweed famous. Even John Terry famous. It was in December 1976 that the Roxy Club opened in Covent Garden, started by McLaren's accountant Andy Czezowski. It used to be a gay club called Shagarama but now it was to be the centre of the punk scene. The 'Studio 54 of punk'.

The Anarchy tour suffered more cancellations than Gatwick when the Icelandic volcano went off. Of the 21 shows originally scheduled by McLaren, they only played seven. The volcano that was John Lydon simmered. 'Anarchy in the UK' entered the Top 30 singles chart despite the cover. The perfect gift for mum for Christmas.

Then it was 1977, the year of the dragon. The IRA were bombing the mainland with London their principal target. It was the year when two sevens clashed – the reggae group Culture released a song about it – an apocalyptic year in many ways.

On 4 January, the Pistols left Heathrow for a mini-tour of Holland. The tabloids ran stories of the group vomiting, spitting and swearing, the usual horror stories; McLaren had released a similar story a few years earlier when he was with The New York Dolls and they were passing through Heathrow. The tabloids just gobbled down anything about the band that he chucked their way. Preferably, it involved bad behaviour like vomiting and swearing, bilious being the key word here, absolutely true to the tabloids' version of the spirit of punk. What actually happened was that Lydon was late and they by-passed the terminal altogether. There is a great picture of them about to board a plane, McLaren wearing an ankle-length fur coat and clutching a little attaché case.

In Holland, the band played the Paradiso in Amsterdam, which looked like the gaffe Al Pacino ran in *Carlito's Way*. Then they played a club in Rotterdam. The audience was tough and spent most of the evening chucking snakebite over their heads in speed-induced dementia. It ended when the Pistols were bottled, and Jones kicked one of the audience in the head as he walked off. Not an agreeable evening.

When the group went back to the Paradiso to play another show, it was the last time that Matlock was to play with the group in that era. The relationship between him and the increasingly irritating Lydon had deteriorated badly. There were immense pressures on the band both internally and externally. McLaren was on record as saying, 'Rotten never had an ounce of musical ability,' whereas he acknowledged that he had brought Matlock in to the band because he was 'an anchor of normality'. How long would it all last was what everybody was asking themselves.

Not long in EMI's view. The story about their alleged exploits at the airport proved to be the final straw and, after high-level talks in the Manchester Square boardroom, the order came down to terminate the contract. A final settlement was reached which saw the band walk away with a total of £50,000 in surplus funds they had wrung from the clammy hands of the corporate giants. Filthy lucre. McLaren had a direct line into the *NME* by then and was feeding them stories every day, upping the ante. Other labels started to chase them, afraid of being left behind but not sure of either the music or the motives behind it, the doubts well founded.

McLaren was in talks with A&M Records about

signing. He had taken along demo tapes of songs to them including 'Pretty Vacant', 'No Feelings' and three different versions of 'Anarchy in the UK', which had stalled at No 27 in the charts. When the EMI deal went down in flames, they had ordered the pressing plants to stop production and the single with the catalogue number EMI 2566 was deleted. Highly collectable, a neglected classic, but the next single that the band were to release was to become even more rare, with only 100 ever made.

Matlock was dropped from the Pistols in February '77. The rumours were flying around for weeks before. A particularly strong one was that Sid Vicious had been auditioned by the band while Matlock was still a member. Matlock himself always stated that McLaren phoned him to tell him to fight for his place in the group. Matlock said that he was not interested any more. They had a meeting in a pub at the back of Oxford Street. Glen said it was in Food For Thought, a vegetarian café near The Roxy. Wherever it took place, McLaren presided and the entire band was present except Lydon. McLaren questioned Matlock as to why he could not get on with the singer, but the bass player had made up his mind. McLaren went away and started firing off telegrams to the media, reproduced here:

GLEN WAS THROWN OUT OF THE SEX PISTOLS I AM TOLD BECAUSE HE WENT ON TOO LONG ABOUT PAUL

MCCARTNEY STOP EMI WAS ENOUGH STOP THE BEATLES WAS TOO MUCH STOP SID VICIOUS THEIR BEST FRIEND AND ALWAYS A MEMBER OF THE GROUP BUT UNHEARD AS YET WAS ENLISTED STOP HIS BEST CREDENTIAL WAS THAT HE GAVE NICK KENT WHAT HE DESERVED MANY MONTHS AGO AT THE HUNDRED CLUB LOVE AND PEACE MALCOLM MCLAREN

Glen went off to form The Rich Kids with Midge Ure, who was hopelessly in awe of the punk phenomenon. McLaren once sold him an amp in Glasgow when Ure was in Slik, one of the first boy bands who never cut the mustard. McLaren had sounded Ure out about joining the Pistols before Lydon had donned his Pink Floyd T-shirt, but McLaren had no need for Ure now. Sid had joined and he was ready to rock the world even further. Young Sid was already jumping up and down very hard on the self-destruct button though. In the course of his talks with A&M, McLaren had told them about the band's next single, a marvellously menacing piece of work, an attack on the monarchy, who his grandmother Rose had brought him up to despise with such intensity. Vivienne Westwood had come up with the idea. They had a working title: 'God Save The Queen'.

CHAPTER 10

'GOD SAVE THE QUEEN'

*'It was having a very damaging effect on the British
political system. I don't think people quite realise –
they were probably the greatest rock'n'roll band in that
sense of going that bit beyond the music and creating the
most amazing uproar in society.'*

MALCOLM MCLAREN

*'Malcolm McLaren: bourgeoisie anarchist.
That just about sums him up.'*

JOHN LYDON

McLaren went for it full tilt now. The Grundy interview had blown the whole scene apart. Strangely enough, a town called Grundy in Virginia was almost washed away in the spring of '77, some sort of biblical revenge, McLaren always thought. What did Michael Caine say in *The Italian Job* to the guy when he demolished the van? 'I only asked you to blow the bloody doors off.' The incident had got them to a place he had dreamed of much quicker than even he could have hoped. The man who sold the famous 'Destroy' T-shirt was looking to destroy the music business.

In February 2010, shortly before McLaren's death, EMI reported a pre-tax loss of £1.75 billion. KPMG issued a 'going concern corner' statement when asked about the stability of the company. The impoverished state of EMI must have been a source of amusement to McLaren in the closing weeks of his life. The short spell the Sex Pistols had with the label did not help their cause. The company that had acts such as The Beatles, Cliff Richard, Pink Floyd and Robbie Williams on their books were struggling as the whole business changed beyond recognition. It was a dinosaur trying to survive in the age of mammals.

In early March 1977, the Sex Pistols signed with A&M Records – the company co-founded by Herb Alpert, an outrageously good-looking fellow who fronted his own Tijuana Brass band in the '60s – for an estimated £50,000. The deal was signed at the offices of Rondor Music. The next day, McLaren restaged the signing outside Buckingham Palace for the benefit of the media, to tie in as a promotion device for the second single, 'God Save The Queen'. It was early in the day and the strung-out Pistols were on edge. A trestle table was hastily erected and the group were snapped signing. It was another iconic photograph, with McLaren wearing a trendy three-quarter-length jacket, all elegance and irony: the complete Soho jazz hipster now the prince of punk. As the band posed for the cameras, McLaren smiled benignly, like he was watching a bunch of rowdy children in a playground. Perhaps he was, the playground being London town and the best address in town: Buck House. Steve Jones said that there had been a fight in the Daimler going to Buckingham Palace.

On 12 March, the record company had a reception for the group in the Speakeasy club in honour of their signing. However, it turned out to be a complete disaster as another ugly incident occurred. 'Whispering' Bob Harris, a radio DJ who also broadcast late-night BBC TV show *The Old Grey Whistle Test*, was in the club. His programme was the complete opposite of the Tony Wilson show that the Pistols had recently been on. If Wilson delivered his show at 100 miles per hour, then Harris's style was at a more sedate pace. If *So It Goes* presented the latest cutting-edge bands like the Pistols, then *The Old Grey Whistle Test* was a haven for the old and grey like Bob Seger and the Silver Bullet Band. Even in those days, 'Whispering' Bob was balding and bearded, a real old hippie clad in denim. When The New York Dolls had been on the show, he had not been overly impressed, turning to the camera after their performance and pronouncing it 'mock rock'.

Sid Vicious started hassling Bob, asking him when the

Pistols were going to appear on the show. Vicious then called Harris 'an old cunt'. Within seconds a free-for-all broke out. Much screaming, shouting and bottle smashing ensued, with tables overturned and mirrors smashed. Vicious, notorious for glassing and cutting, injured both Harris and his pal. It was a nasty injury and he ended up needing 14 stitches in a bad head wound. Harris said he was never so scared. He survived that, though, and a subsequent cancer scare in recent times. 'Whispering' Bob can be found on Radio 2 still playing AOR and Bob Seger records.

There was a backlash against the Pistols from artists like Rick Wakeman of Yes, who wrote in protesting about them and stating he would have to reconsider his position on the label if the Pistols signed. McLaren hated Wakeman's type of music and called him Rick 'Wankman'. McLaren always claimed that he had seen Wakeman's statement, which he said included a phrase about A&M artists 'now having to wear safety pins'. Very droll. Wakeman has appeared on BBC's *Grumpy Old Men* TV show in recent years, although he was a grumpy man over 30 years ago.

It was clear, however, that the Pistols' position on A&M was as untenable as Matlock's had been within the group. Derek Green had been sold the idea of the Pistols by McLaren, thanks to a cassette of the group's latest demos featuring Glen Matlock. It included a classy version of 'EMI', which Green wanted to put out, plus a souped-up version of 'God Save The Queen' that was ready for public consumption. The problem was the Pistols as signed by the label no longer existed. With the benefit of hindsight, McLaren's decision to part from Matlock made no sense. It was tantamount to Sir Alex Ferguson sacking Wayne Rooney and replacing him with one of the stewards who stood around in orange jackets. McLaren always thought that the Pistols would never sell enough records and that his only chance to make serious money was to employ the tactics that had worked so well with EMI.

Sophie Richmond, McLaren's secretary, showed tremendous insight when she spoke to Jon Savage about the situation after the Grundy interview. 'It was a combination of the signing for real money and the Grundy incident, which was the thing that precipitated Glen leaving. Once Glen had left, there were practically no more songs, and that was a problem. Glen could write tunes and they couldn't. They could produce words and chords, but they couldn't write tunes like "Submission". So they were finished as a creative unit once he had gone.'

The writing was on the wall already for the Pistols but they were to burn brightly across the sky before they came crashing down. It was all about tunes in the end, always was, always will be. The year of 1977 saw the release of

Fleetwood Mac's *Rumours* album, while Abba were huge during the whole time this story unfolded. This type of music is still played and sold today, endlessly recycled. A hard but undeniable fact of life in the music business.

The Sex Pistols cut their first A&M single in early March. McLaren tried to get Matlock to sit in on the session but without success. Steve Jones stepped in to help out but it sounded over-produced and, in the end, A&M never released it. Soon after, Green consulted with Herb Alpert and their contract was terminated on 16 March, before a sleeve had even been designed for the single. Legend had it that the company's decision was motivated by the reaction of employees, artists and DJs. The company requested their signing fee back but the Pistols were eventually paid off with an estimated total of £75,000. Derek Green takes full responsibility for the debacle and stated that the man he conducted business with (McLaren) was at the root of it all. He describes McLaren as 'Satanic' and added, 'His manipulation of everyone looks like no fun at all.'

McLaren always claimed total responsibility for the Pistols' antics and that the group deliberately confronted the company because of their bland image. The manager insisted that Green asked him for their money back, but he responded by demanding further cash from them. In a *Melody Maker* article, McLaren explained, 'Green said, "I have something very serious to say to you."

'I knew what it was about, and I was very prepared for it. "We are going to release a press statement saying that we are terminating the contract at six tonight."

'I told them, "You're still going to pay the money."

'They wanted me to help and approve. They did not want to get into a situation like EMI. I did the absolute opposite.'

It had occurred to McLaren that A&M would break up the group but would then try to convince Lydon to stay with them. He always thought that there were talks between them and, after the termination of the group's contract, Lydon would go back to Green and sign a lucrative solo deal. McLaren thought on his feet and decided to take the band to Germany for a holiday. They holed up in the Hotel Kapinsky and McLaren hired a VW microbus so they could do all the touristy things like look at the Berlin Wall. During the holiday, Lydon confided in his old pal Sid and confirmed that A&M had been in talks about a possible deal.

McLaren continued: 'I don't know the truth. I never found out. Sid knew something was happening with A&M. They knew Lydon was the only guy they could speak intelligently to. If they could have taken Johnny and made him feel all right, he would have apologised and rowed us all out. I did not give them a fucking chance.'

Back home, the Pistols played a showcase gig at the Screen on the Green, an independent cinema in

Islington. Vicious had performed competently enough on his earlier debut in the post-Matlock Pistols at the Notre Dame Hotel, but in his second outing he appeared to be totally out of it. Also on the bill were The Slits, a band McLaren saw as the female version of the Pistols, and he had talks with their guitarist Viv Albertine. She remembers McLaren used to arrange to meet her in the strangest of places, like the Gazebo in Soho Square or some obscure Irish pub. It was like in the spy films where the agents would meet in the middle of a park somewhere they could be sure that they were not being followed. Being in Berlin had made him feel like Richard Burton in *The Spy Who Came In From The Cold*. McLaren had an idea for a film for The Slits but it was pretty risqué and nothing ever came of any of it. Slits member Palmolive recalled that when he first met her he stated that he 'hated women and hated music'.

McLaren began telling the press about another film project he had in mind, parodying the Pistols' relationship with the music business. McLaren knew more about getting the maximum out of labels than Trinny and Susannah ever did.

Nick Kent saw this moment as a good time to attack his bête noir. 'The guy [McLaren] has become such a caricature of himself that now it's virtually impossible to see what first motivated him. But there was something real there and it was not just money. He created the name, and he was the guy that held it all together. Most importantly, McLaren did not take drugs at all. So he was always together and that is important.'

Kent made the point about McLaren being free of drugs. When cocaine hit the music business like a hurricane in the late '80s and '90s, virtually everyone in the business was affected. McLaren was always too clever to be involved, which explains how he got so much done and created so many ideas. The critics lined up to take pot shots at McLaren at this time, perhaps because of all the attention he was getting for the two deals he had just pulled off.

Caroline Coon, writer and activist, spoke about Vicious, whose behaviour was becoming increasingly erratic. 'Sid's caught in this maelstrom. Of course he's going to numb his feelings even further with whatever drugs he can, which is classic addict stuff. But his violence is encouraged by people like Malcolm McLaren and Vivienne Westwood ... Sid admired her a great deal.'

McLaren was trying to get another deal going. The Queen's Jubilee celebrations were looming in June and he wanted the single release to coincide with it, and entered into dialogues with American giants CBS and the French company Barclay. CBS eventually dropped out of the hunt, full of misgivings. McLaren was very keen to go with Barclay, as that would necessitate him spending time in Paris. London was becoming too hot even for him, and Paris seemed an ideal retreat. Perhaps he could open a shop out there and annoy the locals.

The name of the shop at 430 King's Road was changed yet again, this time to Seditionaries, towards the end of 1976. McLaren ordered that the shop was to be totally rebuilt and recruited a team of clever young artists to redevelop it. They included Ben Kelly, who was later responsible for designing the Haçienda club in Manchester. 430 King's Road featured opaque white glass. Adam Ant said he preferred it when the jukebox played Vince Taylor records and all the clothes were on a rack on the right. The shop remained Seditionaries until the '80s.

In early May 1977, the band signed for Richard Branson's Virgin Records. It was a significant moment in English pop-music culture because it was a marriage of convenience between the punk and hippie communities: a coalition, and we all know how popular they became. Virgin numbered in its stable ex-folkie Mike Oldfield and off-the-wall bands like Henry Cow, probably not familiar to most readers as they never really made it. Virgin was seen as the last bastion for such bands and McLaren was not pleased, as he saw his punk revolution somewhat diluted. He wanted direct confrontation with dinosaurs like EMI, blue chip, establishment outfits still cranking out slightly ludicrous records. Branson had apparently approached Leslie Hall of EMI at the time of

Grundy-gate with a view to buying up the Pistols' contract. Any chance of that was shot down when mega-bucks A&M stepped in.

Ex-Stowe pupil Branson was hoping that, with the acquisition of Lydon and co, he could attract more punk bands to Virgin. He also saw it as a time to clean house and Henry Cow were put out to grass. Another factor that disturbed McLaren was that Lydon and the gang got on far better with Branson than they ever did with the old spuds Hill and Green. The business mogul came across as open and laidback, a younger, hipper version of 'Whispering' Bob Harris, and the band affectionately nicknamed Branson 'Pickle'. Nicknames were a big thing with Lydon, and when he joined the band he insisted on calling Matlock 'Albert' in homage to *Coronation Street* character Albert Tatlock, another grumpy old man. It infuriated the bass player and added to the tension, but divide and conquer was the name of the game. It always worked better in an unhappy situation, McLaren thought.

Pickle had been persistent and his money was useful. The single had to be out, but McLaren was never keen on signing for Virgin. At that time Branson was seen as being very perceptive and cool, and a few months earlier the two had eyed each other suspiciously across a crowded 100 Club. The Mike Oldfield oilfield was running dry and Branson was looking for another bandwagon to jump on. Aspiration being a lost art, he saw punk as the new pay dirt. Baudelaire informed us that 'Domesticity was the enemy of the artist'. It was also seen by McLaren as being the biggest threat to his vision of the band. The band members were all under 22, and at that stage he thought he could still mould and control them.

'God Save The Queen' soon triggered a host of problems. The staff at Virgin's pressing plant refused to make a pressing plate for the single, and the next day the people involved in the printing refused to work on the sleeve. In both cases, it was only after strong calls from the management that work was resumed and order maintained. It offended the susceptibilities as no other English record had done or would do again; even Frankie Goes to Hollywood's paean to homosexuality, 'Relax', never caused the fuss of McLaren's little ditty.

This was hardly the first time that abuse had been heaped on the Queen. John Osborne, one of the 'Angry Young Men' of the '50s, had written an essay called 'Declaration', in which he attacked the monarchy. 'Waffling cant' was one of the phrases he used. McLaren used to hear people talking about it at Croydon College. Sounded like 'cant' anyway. What the Pistols had come up was comic irreverence, not the righteous indignation of the '50s. Contained in a pop song and beautifully marketed, the message was very clear.

At McLaren's insistence, the band nearly revisited Bill Grundy and the *Today* programme when Virgin tried to place an advert to promote 'God Save The Queen'. Those rotters at Thames Television refused to air it, however, which probably saved a few TV screens from a kicking.

At the end of May, despite another protest at the Virgin pressing plant, the single was released. Released? More like escaped. Cat no VS181 came in the blue and silver picture sleeve that was Jamie Reid's finest hour. The B-side was 'Did You No Wrong', but of course they did. Reid used a portrait of the Queen by Cecil Beaton, lifted, with great irony, from the *Daily Express*. McLaren loved the fact that they sourced their biggest outrage from another pillar of the community. The main design centred around the mouth and eyes of Beaton's portrait. Reid contemplated putting a swastika on to the picture at one stage, but it was just as well it never happened. In the end, they settled for a collage of newspaper type spelling out the title and band's name, printed in the torn strips across the Queen's eyes and mouth. It remains one of the most controversial and best-known record sleeves ever released.

Lydon always remembered the song as a 'bunch of bitterness', scribbled early one morning on his mother's kitchen table. It became the alternative national anthem in Jubilee week but he always maintained it should have been released much earlier, before they signed to A&M. He told Gavin Martin of the *NME*, 'That's how the Pistols worked; everyone would have their own little pieces of nastiness working for them. And like all good songs you keep it short, sharp and to the point.'

MPs called for the record to be banned, with one Labour MP writing in a red top: 'If pop music is going to be used to destroy our established institutions then it ought to be destroyed first.' Destroy: a concept that might look good on a T-shirt.

The BBC banned the single, of course, advising everyone it was 'in gross bad taste'. The Independent Broadcasting Authority issued a warning to all radio stations that the single may be in breach of Section 4:1:A of the Broadcasting Act. The majority of the stations refused even to broadcast the advert for the record. All we got was Radio Ga Ga.

McLaren wrote a press release in response: 'It is remarkable that MPs should have nothing better to do than get agitated about records which were never intended for their Ming vase sensibilities.'

Radio 1 DJ Tony Blackburn said of the record, 'It is disgraceful and makes me ashamed of the pop world, but it won't last.'

Wrong, Tony, old son, because 25 years later Virgin rereleased the song. Both McLaren and John had grown old disgracefully. Tony Blair was in power and the song was arguably as relevant then as it was first time around. You could say the same today.

When the Sex Pistols' boat chugged up the Thames that chilly June night to promote the song, nobody on board ever dreamed that the voyage was going to be almost as famous as when the *Titanic* set sail. The iceberg was looming fast, though.

It would not have been enough for McLaren for the boat just to go up and down the Thames, it had to end in mayhem, some punk *Poseidon Adventure* with the guys dancing on the ceiling. The manager was arrested that night and charged with 'using insulting words likely to provoke a breach of the peace'. Vivienne Westwood was charged with obstruction, and Jamie Reid with assault. Lydon slipped away into the night. He was a fan of the hugely popular TV show *The Fugitive*, about physician Dr Richard Kimble, unjustly accused over murdering his wife. At the end of each show, he would evade capture by the police by just melting away, just as Lydon did now. Soon they were all to be fugitives running for their very lives.

McLaren always upheld that 'God Save The Queen' had reached the No 1 position during the actual Jubilee week and outsold Rod Stewart thanks to the chart compilers including 'advance orders' for 'I Don't Want To Talk About It'/'First Cut Is The Deepest'. Branson always believed that the Virgin single had sold 15,000 to

20,000 more copies that week. The figures from his stores, strangely struck off the weekly census of sales that particular week, indicated this.

For McLaren, the shockwaves from Grundy-gate and the Jubilee outrage were threatening to engulf him. It would need all of his fast thinking to keep afloat.

CHAPTER ELEVEN
NO FUTURE

'They're not scared of you. They are scared of what you represent to them... what you represent to them is freedom. But talking about it and being it – that's two different things. I mean, it's real hard to be free when you are bought and sold in the marketplace.'

JACK NICHOLSON, *EASY RIDER*

'Turn the other cheek too often and you get a razor through it.'

JOHN LYDON

1977 was the prize year for violence. Malcolm McLaren and Richard Branson did not agree on much, but they were both of the same opinion about the Pistols' unfailing skill at shocking the public. In June 1977, public anger came to a pustulant head, the fallout from the fuss caused by the 'God Save The Queen' single causing violence to erupt.

Jamie Reid came off the worst: ironically it was one of his own designs that got him into trouble. He was jumped by a gang of Teds outside a rockabilly pub in

Borough, near London Bridge, while wearing a 'God Save The Queen' T-shirt. The patriotic mob broke his arm and nose, and Reid spent two months in hospital.

John Lydon was the principal target, however, and at one time there were more people looking for him than John Dillinger when he was Public Enemy No 1. He was assaulted twice within three days as the summer of love became one of hate. The first incident happened while he was with producer Chris Thomas outside the Pegasus pub in Islington, when a gang cut him badly and severed tendons in his hand. Lydon recalled that McLaren found it hilarious. A few nights later, Lydon was in Dingwalls when he was attacked again, and they went for his bandaged arm. On this occasion, he escaped thanks to the bouncers, but the attack shocked him to the core, as he finally realised that he was not safe along with the full horror of his predicament. The attacks, the sudden burst of fame, fatigue and amphetamine rage rendering him almost demonic, it all started to really get to him.

Lydon started acting strange, and his version of strange was very strange. He became increasingly withdrawn, hostile and paranoid, muttering about not being a Svengali-directed puppet. McLaren, older, mentally tougher and more experienced, should have stepped in and protected him, nurtured him and stashed him away somewhere safe. A less exploitative manager would have provided adequate security for his singer at the very least. Most days that summer, Lydon didn't have cab fare, just as when he was stranded after the Grundy show.

Paul Cook was walking along Goldhawk Road with his girlfriend when he was jumped by four young Teds. The Pistols' drummer took a battering and was hit hard with some type of metal bar, resulting in a king-sized headache and 15 stitches in his scalp. Cook and Steve Jones were seen as the self-styled hard men of punk, the football hooligans that were in a band at a time when football hooliganism was at its peak, with unprecedented levels of violence. Lydon was quoted at the time as saying that the only 'true anarchists' were football hooligans, but the thugs and the Teds were the ones who decided to mete out the justice that the tabloids were baying for.

In the cinema the Clint Eastwood Dirty Harry movies were showing, while Michael Winner had released the *Death Wish* film just three years earlier, a nasty movie starring Charles Bronson as a vigilante cleaning up the streets after his family had died in a Manson-style slaughter. In possibly his greatest role, Robert de Niro had played the titular *Taxi Driver*, another avenging loner in Martin Scorsese's epic tale about a Vietnam veteran dispensing his own justice to a gang of pimps running an underage prostitute ring. De Niro even shaved his head at the end of the movie and sported a Mohican cut.

All the ingredients for violence were there, shaken and stirred with a ready-made scapegoat, a punk rocker. 'Kill A Punk And Win A Mini' was the spoof headline taken from one of the fanzines, a new publishing culture that sprang up as a by-product of punk. Truly terrifying times, and the music of the Pistols was the soundtrack to it.

One last factor that should never be overlooked was that if you set yourself up as 'a hard man' then you were always going to attract the loonies. Just ask Vinnie Jones. After the Pistols had split, the band that probably courted the most trouble was Oasis, with lead singer Liam Gallagher waging a one-man war against the world. Alan McGee, who signed Oasis to his Creation label, was hugely influenced by the Pistols, and when they re-formed he took out full-page adverts in the music press extolling their virtues.

By now, McLaren saw himself as the true orchestrator of the punk phenomenon. The rules had been changed by him, in his art-school, Situationist, Dadaist way. What it was really about was ripping people off, and McLaren wanted all this to go into a film that was starting to obsess him.

His relationship with Virgin was very complex at this time. They had never met a manager like him before, someone who literally ran the whole show himself. McLaren would have had no time at all for a creative artist, such as James Taylor, for example, who wrote nearly all of his own material. To McLaren, *he* was the creative artist. The tension between him and Lydon increased as the singer started to feel creative himself. He was beginning to write his own songs, not just lyrics, which would later appear in his own post-Pistols band Public Image Ltd.

McLaren was improvising from day to day, torn between the idea of a full-scale tour or guerrilla gigs, one-offs, hitting and running, all the while pretending that the Pistols had been banned everywhere else. In July, he oversaw the release of the band's third single, 'Pretty Vacant', backed with their best ever B-side, a cover of The Stooges' 'No Fun'. The artwork featured the Situationist buses design that Jamie Reid created literally on his way to the Virgin offices. It was his most rushed piece of work but a favourite of McLaren's, who particularly liked the idea of the bus going 'nowhere'. Tickets please.

Much to his chagrin, a film of the single was shown on *Top Of The Pops* a few nights later. It was Branson's idea, the label paying for it to showcase Lydon's ego. In the clip, Lydon is wearing small round dark glasses, modelled on the pair John Lennon wore when he was recording *Revolver*. Lydon wore a long-sleeved muslin shirt with the 'Destroy' logo. The camera lingered on Sid for a second in all his punk glory, clad in his leather jacket and torn jeans. It was an iconic moment for him, caught in aspic, but away from the spotlight his life was out of control. Punk, mainly thanks to McLaren, had given the window of opportunity for the pair to find a place in the world but it was also a two-headed monster that threatened to devour them.

McLaren was stealing another '60s ploy, when all the top groups would churn out hit singles every three months. The jukebox in the King's Road always had a few Stones gems: he recalled when classic hits like 'Satisfaction', 'Get Off My Cloud', '19th Nervous Breakdown' and 'Paint It Black' would just flow seamlessly in those golden summers of '65 and '66. Chrissie Hynde's future husband Ray Davies was another practitioner of this art in the mid-'60s, releasing The Kinks' 'You Really Got Me', 'All Day And All Of The Night' and 'Tired Of Waiting For You' in quick succession.

The 'Pretty Vacant' single made it to No 6 in the chart, despite limited air play. Lydon changed the lyric to 'va-cunt' as the record faded, but nobody really noticed.

McLaren did a great interview with Nick Momus and made the point that, 'It's not the music, it never was, since the Sex Pistols. No one made music because they were interested in music, after the Sex Pistols, they were interested in the process.'

McLaren was full of contradictions, making great play about never being interested in the music, yet, in the space of just over six weeks, he unleashed upon the world two of the most powerful pop statements in its history.

Another split was to occur with John Lydon, though, over musical tastes. In the middle of that sweltering July, Lydon went on Capital Radio with the late DJ Tommy Vance, in a 90-minute show called *A Punk And His Music*. The show started in an interesting manner. It was reported in *Melody Maker* as follows:

TOMMY VANCE: If you could start all over again would you do it exactly the same way?
JOHNNY ROTTEN [As he was known on the show]: Well yeah. It is not as laid out as that. We just did it. Everything we did was spontaneous. I think that is the only way you should do anything because it is honest. If you plan your future it is not such fun. If anything, Malcolm McLaren is the fifth member of the band. What really amuses me about McLaren is the way they say he controls the press, the media manipulator. He's done nothing. He just sat back and let them garble out their own rubbish and they did.
TV: Someone once said he is a fascist.
JR: That's absolute rubbish! He could not be. He's a Jew for a start.

Where Vance got the fascist angle from is not clear, although the tabloids, who totally misread the band from day one, had stupidly tried to link them in with the far-right National Front political party, a forerunner of today's British National Party (BNP). The fact that Lydon referred to McLaren as the fifth Pistol was for public consumption: he was quick to point out that McLaren did 'nothing'. Even then, when everything was happening and both McLaren and Lydon were in the eye of the storm, the argument about who does what was raging.

Lydon went on to play Captain Beefheart and Neil Young, because he considered it to be good honest music, but McLaren thought it was awful. In his view, Lydon was playing crap music by those old American hippies that he despised. Lydon explained in Q magazine: 'I was pulling the rug from under McLaren's schemes and revealing them to be nonsense. That was the end of our loving relationship heeheehee. He thought I was some kind of traitor and he could hardly bring himself to talk to me after that.'

Strange that he chose the term 'loving relationship'. Also, it was self-sabotage because, had the Pistols been exposed as fakes, he had more to lose than anyone. McLaren was always seen as the hustler, but Lydon would have been shown as a complete fraud.

McLaren once spoke to Jon Savage about Lydon's far from promising tastes in music. 'He wanted it all to be fairy-like, like the '60s. Captain Beefheart. He wanted to

Adam Ant and Jordan in 1977.

Above: Bow Wow Wow featured Adam Ant musicians David Barbarossa, Matthew Ashman and Lee Gorman who McLaren set up with singer Annabella Lwin.

Below: The Pistols on their final tour of America with Sid Vicious.

Above: A 1978 news conference in Rio de Janeiro. McLaren behind Steve Jones, actor James Jeter in Martin Bormann Nazi gear, Paul Cook and Great Train robber Ronnie Biggs.   © *PA Photos*

Below: McLaren and Vivienne Westwood facing the press.   © *Rex Features*

Above: McLaren and the World's Famous Supreme Team had a hit in 1983 with 'Buffalo Gals'.

Below: Vivienne Westwood with McLaren.

McLaren had lost none of his energy in the mid-80s as he released 'Soweto'.

Above: Ben Westwood, Vivienne Westwood and her son with McLaren, Joseph Corre. © *PA Photo*

Below: In typical style, McLaren declared he would not go into the jungle for 2007's *I'm a Celebrity… Get me Out of Here!* © *Rex Features*

McLaren and girlfriend Young Kim at a New York fashion show in 2009.

© Getty Images

Above: Malcolm McLaren in 2010.

© *Rex Feature*

Above: The funeral cortege on 22 April 2010. Along with the horse-drawn carriage was a bus going 'nowhere' from Camden to Highgate Cemetery.

© *Rex Feature*

be reggae, 'cos that was in that week. He was a fashion victim in the true sense, a musical fashion victim.'

Then the Pistols went out on the SPOTS tour: 'Sex Pistols On Tour Secretly'. It was McLaren's way of dealing with both the legitimate bans, and the fact that, when not on the road, the band were under his feet, constantly in his office demanding money and causing disruption. He needed to get them away – but working also. In the autumn of that year, McLaren thought that the Sex Pistols were not in the news in the way that he wanted them to be. They should have been but there was nowhere decent for them to play.

One scheme McLaren had was for them to play on common land; he had read up on the legislation and noted that there were no by-laws. He got the idea from a funfair he saw on Clapham Common, near Westwood's home. McLaren even checked out a travelling circus he saw advertised as playing in South London, and decided to go with the fairground idea, pencilling in some dates for summer '78.

The Pistols had been great fans of The Faces, the band fronted by Rod Stewart which also featured Ronnie Wood and the nucleus of The Small Faces, the legendary mod band that some believe were London's greatest ever group. In the early days of The Strand, Matlock, Cook and Jones had cited them as their biggest influence, and at the time they were little more than a Small Faces cover band.

Ronnie Lane was The Faces' ace songsmith, co-writing still-stunning classics like 'Itchycoo Park', 'Tin Soldier' and 'Lazy Sunday', songs that took a chisel to your heart. With Rod Stewart eyeing America and the company of film stars, Lane quit The Faces to tour the country with his own travelling circus. It never made any money but was a brilliant concept that saw Lane in his little caravan travelling from town to town. If McLaren had managed to distil these ideas and actually get the band out into the English countryside with some travelling-circus deal, it would have been brilliant. Sadly, it never happened.

On the SPOTS tour, they used a number of aliases including The Hamsters and The Tax Exiles. Presumably, The Grundys would have blown their cover. How badly hampered they were by bans is again open to conjecture. McLaren always said how hard it was for them to play anywhere. One night when he was in the Music Machine, one of the staff told Lydon that they had been trying for months to get McLaren to commit to a date to play there. Lydon's jaw dropped in amazement and he started to question the things McLaren told him even more closely.

On 16 August, Elvis Presley, the King of Rock'n'Roll, died at the age of 42. Ever prepared to court controversy, Sid Vicious was soon telling everybody that Elvis 'was dead before he died'. Vicious was at pains to point out that he did not want to end up like the bloated, drug-addled star: he wanted to live and 'the music was the thing'. It was a pity he didn't put what he preached into practice, as the tour was marred by his drug taking, posturing and musical ineptitude.

On 15 October, the band's fourth single was released, the stuttering 'Holidays in the Sun' backed with 'Satellite' (Lydon's cruel putdown to Shanne Bradley), in line with McLaren's policy of cranking out the hits one after the other. Lydon had written the drone on tour during the sound checks. Once again the single was the subject of controversy, not so much for the musical content but the artwork again. Reid had customised the artwork of a Belgian tourist brochure. It was very tasteful and, by the band's standards, innocent, but, when the Belgian Travel Service sued, over 60,000 sleeves were withdrawn. Rumour has it that the reverse of the sleeve had been influenced by a Situationist pamphlet printed in Nanterre University.

The single made No 8 in the charts but was not a critical success like its predecessors. It had been written at the time of the band's visit to Berlin, but without Matlock's shrewd songwriting skills it lacked structure. Chris Thomas wanted to put some German 'goose steps' on it somewhere, but settled instead for the skyscraping guitar. McLaren was not concerned; by this time he was deeply involved in the film project. Now he wanted to sell the band as a visual act. Video was to kill the radio star but this was long before MTV and videos became the main tool to market pop stars. Another idea he had was to market them like the Baader-Meinhof Group, a predominantly 1970s German terrorist organisation also known as the Red Army Faction or RDF, with a cocktail of violence and dangerous ideals. Criminals? Revolutionaries? As long as they were notorious, that was all that was required.

The single was a trailer for the album that was released two weeks later, *Never Mind The Bollocks*, and it was the dogs. The band's only kosher album, it rightly made the No 1 spot. The precocity of youth saw them try to outrage still further with the title.

Lydon amusingly recreated the scene of how the album title came about for *MOJO*:

McLAREN [mimicking McLaren's voice as a camp combination of Kenneth Williams and John Gielgud]: What are you going to call it?
LYDON: Dunno.
McLAREN: The Spirit Of '68: The Student Riot Years? McDonald's I Have Burned And Loved?
JONES: Fucking rubbish, never mind the bollocks. Ah – there's the album's title.

The album should have come out much earlier. The problem was McLaren had other, bigger fish to fry. The bulk of his time was spent trying to get a decent film script together and then flying to Hollywood in an attempt to find the necessary finance to make it. He talked to Momus about the album. 'It was an event. It could have been a story; it could have been a movie. It was not a musical landmark. It could not be, you were still presenting the same rock'n'roll chord structures as albums and previous groups had before.

'But what you had was an immense look, a look that unquestionably was going to change the way people were going to think about themselves. A new generation wanted to ally themselves with a new look and this was the new look and it was the look that was the hit. And the new look did not depend on you buying the record. It just depended on you turning your jacket inside out, you know putting your hair up or smashing your shirt and scrawling with Pentel a circle with an A in the middle or wearing a chaos armband.'

Vivienne Westwood wore a chaos armband on the day they buried Malcolm McLaren in Highgate Cemetery. Chaos, always Chaos. Once, when he was small, McLaren spent an hour unpicking the badge off the blazer he hated so much at school. It took him another hour to sew the badge back on upside down. His grandmother stood over him while he did it, later praising her grandson for the neat manner in which he had completed the task.

The title of the album resulted in Chris Seale, manager of the Virgin record store in Nottingham, being arrested for displaying a huge promotion poster for the Pistols. The police enforced part of the 1898 Indecent Advertising Act to trump up charges. Following Seale's arrest, no other stores would touch the posters, and Virgin lost the £40,000 (a great deal of money in those times) the company had spent on in-store promo material. Branson, anxious to out-flank McLaren at every turn, hired some premier-league legal firepower to fight the case. This is why he signed the Pistols, so he could take command in situations such as these, but his heart was still set on an island in the Caribbean. Never trust a hippie. Virgin's defending counsel, the legend that was John Mortimer, brought in a Professor of English to explain the history of the word 'bollocks'. The case was thrown out and the cover ruled to be decent.

That was the difference between the two men: McLaren would have been happier had the record been banned. He did not want to shift units of records in the same way he did not want to sell clothes in 430 King's Road. He wanted the album to be banned while Branson was protecting his investment. Branson became a billionaire, but he was never in McLaren's league.

Christmas Day 1977 found the Sex Pistols playing an afternoon Christmas party at Huddersfield's Ivanhoe Club. The gig was for children of local firemen, the unemployed and single-parent families. Virgin did the catering, as many soft drinks as you could handle, and a huge cake. Like something out of *It's A Wonderful Life*. If George Bailey could have been there doling out cranberry juice to the kids, the picture would have been complete.

McLaren was in a Christmas mood and, in honour of the occasion, wrote on a T-shirt that depicted a cartoon image of street kids: 'They are Dickensian-like urchins who, with ragged clothes and pockmarked faces, roamed the streets of foggy, gas-lit London, pillaging... setting fire to buildings, beating up old people with gold chains and causing havoc wherever they go. Some of those ragamuffin gangs jump on tables amidst the charred debris and the burning torches and play rock'n'roll to the screaming delight of the frenzied, pogoing mob. Shouting and spitting "Anarchy", one of these gangs call themselves the Sex Pistols. This true and dirty tale has been continuing throughout the 200 years of teenage anarchy and so in 1978 there still remains the Sex Pistols. Their active extremism is all they care about and that's what counts to jump right out of the 20th century as fast as you possibly can in order to create an environment that you can truthfully run wild in.'

Imagine some parallel punk twilight zone, another dimension where Bernie Rhodes ignored a green-haired boy wearing a Pink Floyd T-shirt and Richard Hell was lead singer in the Sex Pistols. The unique Englishness of the band would have been completely undermined by Hell's personality. To McLaren, it would have been more Rimbaud, more romantic, more poetic, more French, more European. A case could be made that this was the period of the greatest success in McLaren's career. It was so English, even the repressed sexuality (Grundy-gate had been triggered by the host coming on to Siouxsie). Later on, we had the French-influenced albums – Bow Wow Wow, Adam Ant – all very European, but McLaren has just described the Dickensian street-kids element which was a constant factor, a scene from *The Great Rock'n'Roll Swindle*.

Beautifully written, the Pistols to which the Christmas message is applicable were about to implode. Sid Vicious was the only Pistol true to the ideals of punk, but he was hopelessly addicted to heroin and about to spiral into self-destruction. The gulf between McLaren and Lydon was now a chasm and no bridge ever built was big enough to span it. Steve Jones and Paul Cook just wanted to keep it going; they wanted what they got into the business for: girls and the filthy lucre. In McLaren's view, their ambitions ended at selling out the Nashville, flogging a million records and consorting with bottle-blond euro bimbos.

McLaren's grudging admiration for Steve Jones never diminished; he never said anything that he did not mean or anything that was not precise. On the first night of the SPOTS tour, the band played at the Lafayette Club, Wolverhampton. The audience now were punk 'clones', wearing the Sid uniform of leather jacket, torn jeans, heavy boots and pins, as regimented as the Teds had been at Finsbury Park the night Eddie Cochran played nearly 20 years before. McLaren looked over at Jones and shook his head. Lydon was not pleased with the evening either, the antagonism between him and Sid growing daily, as it had with Matlock.

'Don't expose Rotten,' Jones confided in McLaren. ''Cos if you expose his shortcomings the whole thing would blow up.'

It was chillingly accurate, and the forthcoming trip to the US in the New Year was to show McLaren exactly how much so.

CHAPTER 12

WHO KILLED BAMBI?

'I started at the top and worked my way down.'
ORSON WELLES

*'Be childish, be irresponsible, be disrespectful,
be everything society hates.'*
MALCOLM MCLAREN

McLaren loved the movies, so much so that in some of his tributes he was compared to Orson Welles, the greatest maverick of them all. At the age of just 26, Welles made one of the greatest movies of all time, *Citizen Kane* (the 'Rosebud' riddle that ran through the movie was mimicked in *The Great Rock'n'Roll Swindle*'s 'Who Killed Bambi?' question).

Years later, McLaren met Orson Welles in Hollywood. Welles was approaching the end of his life and looking back on his career with regret. Having started off early in his career with *Citizen Kane*, it was all downhill. He was reduced to doing voiceovers in cheesy TV show *Magnum PI* and advertising lager. He did not want the same thing to happen to the well-spoken Englishman with the red hair.

McLaren had the idea of making a film called *Who Killed Bambi?* after the *Today* show with Bill Grundy. Imagine harnessing the effect that appearance had on the nation into a film. To McLaren, rapidly tiring of the record business, the idea was an attractive prospect. Virgin was harder to deal with than EMI or the Americans and like the old song says there was no future in the record business. The Pistols were like nitroglycerine, and Vicious and Rotten were rocking the boat too hard. If only he could somehow manipulate the film business as he had music.

The problem was, his infatuation with the idea of a Pistols film would ultimately destroy the band as surely as Sid's infatuation with Nancy Spungen would destroy him.

The full story of *Who Killed Bambi?* – the film eventually released as *The Great Rock'n'Roll Swindle* – is so complicated it could fill up most of this book. It had four directors and eight scriptwriters. McLaren wanted it to be his *Citizen Kane* or, for students of cinema, Warren Beatty's *Reds*. What he did not want was for it to be a pop film like The Beatles' first movie *A Hard Day's Night*, a movie he despised. But he did want his film to be a blockbuster.

Russ Meyer, a Hollywood legend who had made 30 soft-core porn movies, was chosen as the director. His most famous film, *Beyond The Valley Of The Dolls*, about the porny adventures of a girl rock group, was considered at one time to be the follow-up to *Valley Of The Dolls*, the film of the book that had inspired The New York Dolls. *Valley Of The Dolls* author Jacqueline Susann hated the sequel so much she ended up suing the director. It was packed with the voluptuous girls that were Meyer's trademark. Steve Jones loved the movie and had recently been to see it at the Electric Cinema in Notting Hill.

McLaren had flown to Hollywood in July 1977 to meet Meyer; he was wearing his favourite 'Destroy' T-shirt and leather trousers. Meyer had a fantastic bright-red Cadillac, like the one The Clash drove around New York. Together they drove to a building off Sunset and Vine, an area where most buildings look like homes but in fact few are. This is no exception: it was a recording studio owned by a friend of McLaren's. There they watched the Pistols on the Grundy show and listened to *Never Mind The Bollocks*. McLaren proudly boasted that the language used was the filthiest ever heard on British television. Unfortunately, the pair didn't get on, McLaren seeing the army-trained Meyer, who had shot combat footage for the US Army as a newsreel cameraman during World War II, as some sort of crypto-fascist. Meyer saw McLaren as a good way of obtaining money so he could make another porn film. That was how he operated, and with the advent of video and later DVD he made millions on his trashy films as he always retained the rights.

Johnny Speight, creator of the Alf Garnett character in *Till Death Do Us Part*, had been approached to do the first script. McLaren hated it and decided to employ John Varnom, who worked for Richard Branson. Together they cooked up a script that McLaren took to Hollywood in his leather briefcase, but Meyer loathed it so much he brought in a young Dutch director called Rene Daalder to do a rewrite. Daalder had enjoyed a hit with the prophetic *Massacre at Central High* and had written, with Luis Buñuel, *The Discreet Charm of the Bourgeoisie*.

McLaren locked himself away with Daalder to work on the script. Each night Meyer would hold a meeting to monitor their progress, and it soon became apparent that this arrangement was not going to work. Eventually, Meyer chucked the completed screenplay into the bin.

In desperation, Meyer turned to his friend Roger Ebert, who had written *Beyond The Valley Of The Dolls*. Ebert was a real hot shot, dubbed 'the fastest typewriter in Hollywood'. Each day he would write while McLaren and Meyer went out to business meetings at 20th Century-Fox, trying to cut a deal on the film. Meyer wanted the whole script finished and pushed hard for it.

Ebert said McLaren seemed unconcerned, as if screenplays wrote themselves. McLaren contributed to the script though; he specified that he wanted a scene with Sid taking drugs with his mother as well as a sexual liaison between them. Meyer, no prude, queried such an inclusion, but McLaren insisted that it was based on fact. Sid would be OK with it, he claimed.

Eventually, Ebert completed a script called *Who Killed Bambi?*, a spoof on the Disney film. McLaren loved it. Ebert had written a racy Hollywood version of London in the sort of caricatured way only Tinseltown could do, like when they would shoot an episode of *Columbo* in London with the really old red buses and everybody speaking like David Niven. The Pistols were blown up to be larger than life, which took some doing. Art imitating life, almost. Vicious was portrayed as a psychopath, whereas Cook and Jones were extensions of their lager-swilling, girl-chasing selves, pre-dating the *Loaded* lads' magazine culture which chimed with Oasis and Britpop in the '90s. Lydon was shown as moody, aggressive burned-out rock star BJ, an amalgam of Kris Kristofferson in *A Star Is Born* and Mick Jagger as Turner in *Performance*. The character was even originally called MJ, after Mick Jagger. Fearing Jagger's lawyers, it was changed to BJ. Michael Jackson was still only on the first cusp of superstardom; having made his name with The Jackson 5, he was yet to soar to the top as a solo star. The initials MJ would have been even more relevant two decades later.

McLaren's own character was a clever satire on himself, called PT Boggs. 'Fancies himself as the nation's leading and most uncanny trend spotter', was the quote. In the opening scene, McLaren describes how BJ, dressed like Russell Crowe in *Robin Hood*, kills a young girl's pet deer. This was the only scene shot for *Who Killed Bambi?* that was salvaged for the eventual movie.

Russ Meyer blew into London in August 1977 with the nubile Ann-Marie, star of his latest film *Beneath The Valley Of The Ultra Vixens*. Cook and Jones immediately bonded with him... he was their kind of guy. Jones's admiration increased even further when he learned that the star of *Beyond The Valley Of The Dolls*, former model Edy Williams, had been once been Mrs Russ Meyer. Meyer hired a house in Cheyne Walk, a few doors down from where the original MJ, Mick Jagger, had lived with his first wife Bianca. Marianne Faithfull had previously lived there with Jagger when they had been pop's golden couple. Faithfull was supposed to be in the film, playing Sid's mum.

When McLaren approached Ann-Marie to play a part in the film, Meyer was horrified: it was OK to churn this trash out, but for her to actually deal with these types was strictly taboo. One can imagine what type of role McLaren had envisaged for her.

Vicious and Lydon, broke and feeling increasingly isolated, were not keen on the idea of a movie at all. Sid was becoming more and more hooked on heroin and his relationship with Nancy Spungen was already strained. Naturally suspicious, Lydon was wary of Meyer and McLaren's movie plans. He told Jon Wilde about his feelings. 'McLaren was more involved in his artistic ideas than any lust for money. And I hated the film, it was an appalling idea right from the start.

'I was disgusted by things when they got that idiot American.'

The American idiot, Meyer, took Lydon out for a meal after telling him that he looked like he had not eaten for weeks. They went to an expensive restaurant in Beauchamp Place at the back of Harrods. Lydon confirmed Meyer's observation about his eating. 'That fucker McLaren does not pay us anything,' he told the director. 'He gives us an allowance of £5 a week. I am living in a doss house.'

Meyer told Lydon that he would not have lasted a day in the US army as a dog soldier. 'What would I have wanted to be in the fucking army for?' came the singer's reply. Meyer reminded John that America won the Battle of Britain for him, a strange remark considering that America was not even in the war at the time the air battle raged above London in 1940.

Meyer grew suspicious of McLaren's finances and

expressed his concerns to Ebert. His basic fee was £30k, according to McLaren, but part of the deal was that he was paid weekly and the funds had not always been paid on time.

Costs were spiralling because of the rewrites. McLaren, new to the film game, had no idea of a film's true costs, and as they rose he became increasingly upset. He even had an idea about trying to include Elton John in the film somewhere to boost its commercial value.

20th Century-Fox had originally budgeted the film at £150, 000 and had invested most of the money in it. That was until the head of production, Alan Ladd Jr, decided to pull the plug. Ladd, married to Cheryl, who had replaced Farrah Fawcett in the original *Charlie's Angels* show, decided the combination of the maverick porn-filmmaker and the crazy Limey pop band was too much of a risk for him to commit to. Fox had made money on *Beyond The Valley Of The Dolls* but this was uncertain. With the huge success of *Star Wars*, family entertainment was the new buzz word, and the Sex Pistols could hardly have been considered this.

McLaren later put about a story that Princess Grace of Monaco, soon to die in a car smash, was a major shareholder in the company and she had personally vetoed the project, appalled at the thought of a punk group making a movie for the company.

Good Ol' Boy Meyer was also disillusioned that the

Pistols were not as tough as he had been led to believe. He expected tough guys but got a junkie and some paper tigers. Lydon was, in his view, 'a prima-donna asshole'. Meyer never got to film the Pistols. The company's bean counters calculated that the true budget figure would have risen to a figure in the region of £750,000. The financial problems placed an insupportable burden on the relationship between Meyer and McLaren, and in September Meyer shot the deer-killing sequence and then departed London. Lydon claimed that alone had cost £70,000 and that they had made most of it up as they went along. A potential masterpiece was troubled by the chaos of its production and finances.

When *The Great Rock'n'Roll Swindle* finally appeared, Meyer completely dissociated himself from the film and got in the queue to sue McLaren. He told *Melody Maker*, 'There were too many problems in the end. It was my kind of film – very fast paced. It would have been funny, outrageous, a very high grosser. So it was a very big emotional letdown for me at the time.'

Meyer continued to make his movies. He died in 2004 following complications of pneumonia.

In his account of what went wrong, McLaren claimed 20th Century-Fox read the screenplay and pulled the plug. This seemed unlikely to Meyer because the studio would have read the screenplay before giving it the go-ahead rather than torpedoing it afterwards. Roger Ebert claimed that Meyer phoned him to say McLaren had made false promises of financing and was broke, and electricians had walked off the set after not being paid.

With Meyer back in Hollywood, McLaren had to come up with another director. There was a rumour that he approached Julia Phillips (the first woman producer to win an Oscar, with *The Sting*) but nothing came of it. Phillips was later to write her brilliant Hollywood confessional *You'll Never Eat Lunch In This Town Again* after battling cocaine addiction.

Jonathan Caplan, who had made *White Line Fever* for Roger Corman, wrote a script entitled *Anarchy In The UK*, which dealt with a 'Pistols Park' in memory of a pop group 'removed' by the government. The investors rejected it. McLaren liked the writing but commented that the author had made, in his opinion, the mistake of 'falling in love with Rotten'.

Peter Walker, a British director of sensationalist horror films, such as *The House of Whipcord*, was next to throw his hat into the ring. Walker's idea was to do a spoof on *A Star Is Born* and call it *A Star Is Dead*. McLaren liked the idea so much that shooting was pencilled in to commence at the end of February 1978, when the Pistols had returned from their American tour. It never happened, though...

Rotten had left the Pistols by then in an attempt to try to reclaim the soul of John Lydon. What was left of the

Pistols were now working with Warners after leaving Virgin. As part of the original deal, McLaren had skilfully arranged for them to invest £200,000 in the *Who Killed Bambi?* project, and the company saw the film as a good way of breaking Johnny Rotten in the States. But the problem was that the States had broken Johnny.

McLaren was still working with the all-girl group The Slits, now signed to Island Records. He had developed a slot for them in the original *Bambi* film, involving them wearing masks and little else at one of Andrew Logan's parties. Russ Meyer would have approved. McLaren maintained that Chris Blackwell, the Island boss, had offered him £100k upfront to manage The Slits and make a film with them.

Hindsight is a wonderful thing. If McLaren had walked away from the Pistols, now languishing below the water line and going down quickly, and joined up with The Slits, the whole of pop music might have taken another direction. McLaren always thought there was a huge market for a properly managed girl pop group. This was almost 20 years before The Spice Girls hit the scene. The Slits, however, were not overly keen on the proposed movie, pure Russ Meyer stuff about a girl group sold by the white slave trade to work in Mexico.

McLaren, meanwhile, still clung to some vague hope that he could finish the *Bambi* project and even reconcile with Lydon. In a rare moment of reflection, he admitted to *Melody Maker*, 'I thought at the time the film might, just might, induce Rotten to change his mind. I am afraid I was very stupid. I was never ruthless enough. I should have never done that. I should have stayed with The Slits, gone off to Mexico and made that fucking film with them.'

That was McLaren: all heart, not ruthless enough.

In the end he went with the Pistols/Warner project. His first idea was just to make a documentary film about the group. He enlisted the aid of former Cambridge student Julien Temple, who had worked for McLaren's Glitterbest organisation and filmed the antics of the Jubilee boat trip. That could have made a movie in itself, but McLaren was not keen on expanding the project at that stage. Exhausted by events in America, he had mixed feelings about even working with the remaining Pistols as his enthusiasm dwindled. Working with Temple, however, rekindled his desire to make a proper movie. The half-completed film about Oxford Street that he had worked on in his student days still haunted him. Soon he was working till 3am with Temple on a new movie script.

Temple spoke to the *Observer* about the original concept of the movie shortly after McLaren's death. '*The Great Rock'n'Roll Swindle* was conceived at the height of the Pistols' fame to incense and confuse all those Sex Pistols fans who had begun to kneel down beneath posters of the band on their bedroom walls. The point of the Pistols was to destroy that culture of celebrity subservience and inspire kids to get up and do it themselves.'

The Temple/McLaren version now seemed to acknowledge that, with Rotten no longer in the group, the halcyon days of the Sex Pistols as a threat to society had passed. By the end of the film, Vicious and Cook are killed off in road accidents, while Jones is portrayed as burned out by his lifestyle and the pressures of fame.

McLaren himself is alive at the end of the film, a strange, sinister figure locked away in 430 King's Road obsessed by the band and their history. Perhaps his greatest fear was to end up like that. Philip K Dick's *Man In The High Castle* said it all. What McLaren was trying to say was that, unlike bands like The Rolling Stones who continue to maintain their commercial position, the Pistols would self-destruct to maintain their relevance. That is why McLaren was so disappointed when the Sex Pistols re-formed in the '90s, in his mind a pale imitation of what they had stood for in 1977 when they had taken on the world and, for an all-too-brief period, won. In the end of David Bowie's best movie, *The Man Who Fell to Earth*, his character, the alien Jerome Newton, is a hopeless drunk seduced by the world and all its temptations. He has betrayed everything he stood for at the start and has failed in his mission to save his people from extinction.

The footage of Meyer's *Who Killed Bambi?* is brilliantly weaved into the plot of the final movie: the killing of Bambi by the decadent pop star is avenged by the little girl whose pet it was. The message is now very clear: punk rock and its children have turned on us. Julie Burchill told us we were all the children of 'Thatcher and McLaren after all'.

Rather rashly, Temple told the tabloids that Meyer had personally shot a deer with a pistol (not Vicious) on that first day. Meyer sued for libel, insisting that he just wanted to clear his name, that he did not 'go around shooting deer with pistols'. Temple had to purchase a full-page ad in *Screen International* to apologise. Maybe that's why Meyer never got to direct De Niro and Christopher Walken in *The Deer Hunter*.

As the film closes, a *Guardian* reporter (another organisation that McLaren despised because of its liberalism) asks McLaren, 'Is punk rock dead?'

McLaren replies, 'That is the most laughable statement I have heard this year. Who killed Bambi?'

The structure of *The Great Rock'n'Roll Swindle* is contained in the ten lessons that McLaren ("The Embezzler') delivers at strategic moments. They not only help to explain the history of the Pistols, but McLaren wanted there to be rules a new band could use as they made their way in the record business. Not that anybody does much any more.

Among McLaren's 'rules' are: 'Remove any members of the group who show signs of any developing musical ability. Replace them with gimmicks designed purely to upset people' and 'Find yourself a lawyer who has no interest in music, but is purely interested in making money. He is your main asset.'

The film posed three main questions: what were the motives of the group; why did the media and general public hate the band so much; and what happened to them afterwards?

Perhaps surprising to many is the vital part played in the Sex Pistols by Steve Jones who, other than McLaren, has the most important part in the film. In the film, he is dressed as a private eye, rather in the manner McLaren was the night he was supposed to meet Guy Debord in The Man In The Moon (now sadly boarded up and earmarked to reopen as another plush wine bar).

McLaren was on the case that night, trying to crack the mystery of the situationist, Jones is the same in the film, endlessly walking a Soho back alley at night, just strolling aimlessly but recalling in his mind all his times in the Pistols. McLaren explained once that he wanted to convey Jones as dying in a way and watching his life flash by. In one of the most violent crime films of the '60s, *Point Blank*, Lee Marvin played the part of Parker, a criminal also retracing his life as he tries to recover his share of a robbery in which he was badly injured. At the end, we are not sure if Parker is a ghost or not: the same could be said for Jones in *Swindle*.

Vicious does not figure much, except for his famous scene where he performs 'My Way' (Temple wanted him to record the Edith Piaf song 'Je Ne Regrette Rien' (No Regrets)). At the end of the song, he pulls a gun and shoots his mother. McLaren was drawing on a lot here, his relationship with Vicious's mother, the late Anne Beverley, was, like his relationship with his own mother, not a good one. Perhaps the shooting scene, filmed in the Screen on the Green, was his way of bringing some closure to the relationships.

The Rotten/Lydon character is restricted to footage in Temple's earlier documentaries. At the start of the film, an effigy of him hangs from a gallows and is then burned by the 18th-century version of punks, a throwback to the Gordon Riots and the Dickens Barnaby Rudge images which studded McLaren's work.

The most striking image, however, is that of a woman journalist, a representation of Caroline Coon. She attacks Steve Jones at a record company do. This is a direct reference to Jones's loutish behaviour at the A&M party to welcome the Pistols on to the label. They trashed the place and Jones copped off with one of the secretaries, and later Vicious attacked 'Whispering' Bob Harris and his mate in the Speakeasy. Coon was a virulent critic of McLaren over the years (after an outcry about the Pistols' use of swastikas, she once told Jon Savage that she was suspicious of Jews like McLaren being anti-Semitic). McLaren took his revenge with the images of 'parasitical ants' crawling all over her face. This was a direct steal from Luis Buñuel's *Un Chien Andalou*, the 1929 surrealist film which included footage of an eye being cut with a razor blade. It was also used by David Bowie, who screened the film instead of using a warm-up act on his 1976 'Station To Station' world tour.

The Great Rock'n'Roll Swindle was supposed to be McLaren's masterpiece, but it was sadly neglected and badly received. Even McLaren never seemed happy with it, but, considering the circumstances it was created under and its tortuous progress, it could have been treated in a far better manner. Perhaps this will go some way to re-evaluating it. After all, if they are running university courses on *The Wire*, then surely *Swindle* deserves some praise.

Leave the last word to McLaren, who at one point in the film turns to the camera and mutters in best Michael Caine style the aside: 'If people bought the records for the music, the scene would've died years ago.'

CHAPTER 13

WHO KILLED NANCY?

'I've met the man in the street and he's a cunt.'
SID VICIOUS

'I did feel very, very upset about Sid and Nancy. I particularly spent a great deal of time and money trying to save Sid against the band's wishes, something I later paid for in court. I can't help thinking sometimes how Johnny Rotten, and later Steve Jones and Paul Cook, had so little compassion for Sid. I guess it was a moment when everyone became far too self-obsessed.'
MALCOLM MCLAREN

'Nancy was such a slob, the way she walked and flopped about.'
VIVIENNE WESTWOOD

Nick Kent wrote that the first time Sid Vicious took heroin was not in the company of his girlfriend Nancy Spungen, but when he was hanging out with two of The Heartbreakers, Johnny Thunders and the drummer Jerry Nolan. All three are now long since dead from drug abuse.

Vicious was sick when he first tried the drug and was

not at first taken with the substance. When Spungen came to town to try to rekindle her affair with Nolan, she eventually hooked up with Sid, and the rest, as they say, was history. They would have first met shortly after Vicious had officially joined the band and attended the A&M signing at Buckingham Palace.

Nancy Spungen was the product of a middle-class family who lived in the Philadelphia suburbs. If they had lived in England, they would have been the sort of folk who read the *Daily Mail* and would have been shocked at the *Today* programme had they had occasion to watch it the night Queen could not appear. It was clear from early on that Nancy, their eldest daughter, was a highly disturbed child, medicated from just a few months old to stop her constant crying and hyper behaviour. She had her first psychiatric evaluation at four in a bid to check her wild mood swings and terrible temper tantrums.

If McLaren was having problems with *Jane Eyre* in his troubled childhood, then Nancy was struggling to get to grips with the uneasy works of Sylvia Plath. Spungen was always interested in the manner of her death. Early death fascinated her, just as Eddie Cochran's death had been a landmark event in the formative years of McLaren. The rest of her childhood was text book – or more like horror-comic book – stuff. Sent to a home for disturbed children, she took acid, got into Hendrix and tried to cut her wrists.

Spungen had an abnormally high IQ and at 16 won a place at the University of Colorado. For a short while, it looked as though she had her life back on track but was booted out for stealing from her classmates. She abandoned the idea of studying and turned to music, where she became a groupie. It was the mid-'70s and glam and heavy rock still ruled the roost: Queen, Aerosmith and the appropriately named Bad Company were among the bands she went after. One day, Nancy's mother Deborah, who wrote a moving book about her daughter's tragic life, came home to find her daughter 'entertaining' our old friends The Pretty Things.

Spungen soon left home for New York City intending to make a name for herself in the music business, and I suppose you could say she did in a way. Her first gainful employment, however, was in a topless bar. It sounds like something out of a Lou Reed song. Soon she was dyeing her hair blonde and hanging out with the most famous one in town, Debbie Harry. It was an exciting time for music as the new wave swept all before it, and Spungen was frequenting its major haunts, Max's Kansas City and CBGB's. She was rumoured to have had a fling with Richard Hell, always McLaren's preference for the Pistols' singer's job.

Nick Kent described Spungen as a hardcore groupie and she was soon an accomplice of the woman considered to be the number-one groupie of the day,

Sable Starr. Spungen soon absorbed Starr's myriad stories of her conquests of the cream of the rock world. When she finally landed in London, these tales now featured her in the Starr (as opposed to star) role. She was soon soliciting punters at Piccadilly to pay for Sid's and her heroin habit.

Together, Sid and Nancy and heroin were a lethal combination and McLaren quickly realised that he had to separate them for the sake of the band's future.

'Sid had shot up speed before and got off it,' Vivienne Westwood told *Melody Maker*, 'but he was not shooting heroin at all until he had been with Nancy for a little time. Soon after they were both junkies. What she reminded me of was a gangster's moll who continually flatters her bloke, buttering up his ego all the time, and everybody else around him knows that she has got her hooks into the right thing for the time being. So that is what they were like.

'Really what she did was feed Sid's weaknesses to the extent that other people could not communicate with him. Everybody got fed up trying to relate to Sid, they wanted to but they could not.'

The comparison has already been made between Vivienne and McLaren and Bonnie and Clyde, but Sid and Nancy were closer. Like the Barrow Gang, they both died violent deaths after causing mayhem and disrupting the order of things. Vicious's heroin habit always seemed to be prompted as much by bravado as from any deep-rooted neurosis. Any psychologist would tell you that the origin is the same: the same bravado that Clyde Barrow displayed when he introduced Miss Bonnie Parker to the teller before he robbed the bank, and started shooting. The same bravado that Sid Vicious/Simon John Ritchie/Simon Beverley displayed when he shot up with Johnny Thunders for the first time.

McLaren hatched a plan to try to split them up by kidnapping Spungen. With Vicious at the dentist for treatment on a troublesome molar, McLaren tried to get her into a Heathrow-bound car. They had promised her a free holiday back in the Big Apple, but when she realised that it was just one way she kicked off. Some of McLaren's staff tried to bundle her into the vehicle but Spungen was a tough little cookie if nothing else.

One night the pair went to Lydon's new home at 45 Gunther Grove, just a short distance from Seditionaries. Since he'd been attacked, Lydon spent most of his time there, shut up, getting up very late, holding odd parties, drinking. Typical rock-star burn-out behaviour, John was becoming BJ as written in the original script of *Who Killed Bambi?*. McLaren had less and less time for the punk hobgoblin and took this as a sign of his increasing paranoia and general decline. Vicious said he had gone for a chat to clear the air, but it was more likely that he wanted to score some drug money. Lydon ignored him and after awhile, Sid being Sid, he tried to kick down the door. Lydon had some mates stationed in the house for protection, a bit like Elvis and his Memphis Mafia. A couple of them were real headbangers, football hooligans that had 'done a bit' in prison. Today, they would have had Rottweilers barking on short leashes. One of them rushed out with an axe and took a swing at Vicious. He ducked but Spungen copped it and spent two days in hospital.

In early January 1978, the Pistols set sail for America, their last voyage together. A few months earlier, they had signed to Warner Brothers, part of the huge WEA conglomerate, in the hope of cracking the massive American market. McLaren had cleverly kept this away from Branson and Virgin. The US company was anxious to release 'Pretty Vacant' as their first Stateside single, with a plan to launch them in America with a show in the 20,000-seat Madison Square Garden in New York, scene of many a punch-up in the ring and out. The idea was to reduce the admission charge to a mere $2 to enable the financially challenged punks access to the event. McLaren fought the idea immediately, as he felt a big gig like that would highlight the band's weaknesses. He also thought it would prove to be an anti-climax – which was the thing he feared most.

From day one, McLaren fought with Warners; on his agenda was a hope that somewhere down the line they would fall out and he could walk away with some eating money and more headlines. At first, visa problems arose because of the criminal records of three of the group. Nothing heavy, but Jones was a borstal boy and Lydon and Vicious had minor drug convictions. This was decades before 9/11 and today they would probably be arrested on the spot by some Jack Bauer types.

McLaren thought of another wheeze and applied to play in Russia, an idea that had been fermenting in his mind since convincing The New York Dolls to wear red leather and play with the hammer and sickle flag behind them. He informed the Russian embassy that the Pistols were anti-American and would love to play a gig in Moscow.

1978 was another year of violence and mayhem, nothing new really. Pope John Paul died after just 33 days of papacy. Keith Moon, drummer of The Who, another of the Pistols' favourite bands, died of an accidental drug overdose. Serial killers were big news, as they always were in America. Richard Chase, the Vampire of Sacramento, was captured after murdering six people in a killing spree that shocked the whole country. Chase was called the Vampire because he drank the blood of his victims. He did this in a delusion that he had to prevent Nazis from turning his blood into poison. Chase told police that the Nazis had placed poison under his soap dish. Sid and Nancy followed the case with great interest and read everything they could find on it. They would have also been aware of the fact that the Son of Sam killer was sentenced to 365 years: should be out about 2343 if he behaves himself.

As things were getting interesting, US visas came through after effective lobbying by Warner Bros. Hostility against the band had already been stirred up by *Time* and *Newsweek*, both magazines picking up the bad 'Filth and the Fury' vibes against the Pistols in the British press. Soon they were being deemed a threat towards moral decency and a threat to young persons like Nancy Spungen. The Pretty Things seemed to have been exempted from this criticism.

McLaren compared the situation to that of American comic Lenny Bruce, who was deported from England in the '60s. McLaren was a big fan of Bruce, without whom there would have been no Bill Hicks, the great American stand-up comedian who died at 32 of cancer. Rock'n'roll had been the natural home for such spirits, but so was comedy. All three men were in a renegade class of their own, enemies of boundaries, disturbers of the peace and capable of great insight. None of them got fat, or rich, or were frightened to speak out. Boys will be boys.

The American tour was McLaren's last great adventure with the Pistols, if you did not take the Ronnie Biggs scam too seriously, but he had to fight Warners over the tour dates. Recalling the trouncing The New York Dolls had taken at the hands of the critics, he had no desire to play New York. He wanted the less glamorous cities in the Deep South where he hoped the Pistols' notoriety would provoke trouble. It had worked so well in England, so why not here?

McLaren had planned it so well. The original tour schedule was that they would play the black strongholds of Birmingham and Selma, Alabama, Shreveport in Louisiana, and then on to Tupelo, the birthplace of Elvis Presley. How many years had it been since McLaren had strolled down the King's Road wearing the blue lame suit, a copy of the gold one designed by Nudie's of Hollywood and worn by the great man on the cover of *50,000,000 Elvis Fans Can't Be Wrong*? He wanted to do an EP one day using the artwork and putting Vicious out doing some really old Elvis stuff, 'Baby Let's Play House' for example. 50,000,000 Sid fans and all that. Vicious had worn a gold lame jacket he bought in Kensington Market the night he played at the Screen on the Green.

The tour started off in an Atlanta shopping mall where they played in a 500-capacity concert hall. Warners had to post a $1 million surety against the Pistols' behaviour and had bodyguards to look after Vicious, suffering from acute heroin withdrawal. Spungen, not allowed on the trip, was left behind in London. McLaren was also in London on film business but he joined up with the tour for the second date in Memphis before contracting a really bad cold. The group went on stage an hour and a half late, and were pelted with paper cups. Vicious was uncontrollable by now, gashing his arm with a knife and fighting with the audience. He kept taunting the audience, jeering at their long hair and flared jeans. That far south, there were very few real punks, just hippies, red necks and cowboys.

It got worse at Randy's Rodeo in San Antonio, a true Wild West town that used to figure heavily in those gunfighter songs sung by Marty Robbins. Vicious had 'Gimme a fix' scrawled across his chest and called the audience 'cowboy faggots'. Fights and scuffles broke out throughout the show, with a gang of Mexicans fighting with the cowboys. The crowd literally threw everything they could get their hands on – bottles, hot dogs, popcorn – it just rained down on the band. Eventually, the sheriff came on stage and was hit by a bottle of Jack Daniel's, and at one point it looked like he was going to go for his guns and start firing into the crowd. By now, McLaren admitted that Vicious would 'kill him' were he to try to rein him in and, sensing real danger, the manager backed away from the bass player.

Two days later, on 10 January 1978, the Pistols played the Longhorn Ballroom, Dallas, once a topless bar owned by Jack Ruby, the man who killed Lee Harvey Oswald. It was a tough venue, and that night saw the worst violence of the tour so far when 1800 fans packed into the venue. Lydon had the flu and a very high temperature. Vicious had been drinking all night, still craving heroin, and was butted in the face by a punk girl who had travelled from San Francisco to catch the show. Covered in blood and with no shirt, the picture of him on stage became another iconic image. The British press were giving it extensive coverage, though McLaren was trying to keep it as low profile as possible.

Later on, Vicious stabbed himself in the chest with his weapon of choice, the broken beer bottle. Sid had now eclipsed Lydon as the central figure in the band, all eyes on him, wondering what he would do next, with even Jones subdued around him, watchful, cautious. McLaren became increasingly paranoid as the tour continued, worn down by the travelling and the violence, convinced that the CIA were following the band and bugging their phones. He was more than likely correct.

Perhaps the most famous show the Pistols ever gave was their last one with John Lydon, on 14 January 1978 at the Winterland Ballroom, San Francisco. Compared to the fun and games down in San Antonio, it was as orderly and serene as the Chelsea Flower Show. Vicious did his best to disrupt the performance, chucking his shirt away, playing the wrong songs, gobbing at everybody and generally being an all-round bad egg.

The venue, an old skating rink, was converted into a venue by Bill Graham, the famous promoter most closely associated with the Fillmore Auditorium hippie haven of the '60s. The last song the Sex Pistols ever played together was Iggy Pop's 'No Fun', with some blistering guitar from Steve Jones. Lydon had turned it in by now. The flu could not have helped. Near the end of the song he informed the audience that it was literally 'No fun, No fun, It is no fun at all.'

The crowd must have got the message but then Lydon leaned into the mic and uttered the immortal goodbye: 'Ever get the feeling you've been cheated?'

So that was how it ended. Not with a bang but a whisper. McLaren just went on being McLaren: what else could he do? Jones and Cook flew down to Rio to link up with Ronnie Biggs, McLaren's greatest statement but sadly misjudged by most and only really appreciated by his staunchest and most tuned-in fans. Lydon went back to Chelsea to form PiL and act out the cartoon punk he is still to this day. Vicious ended up in the Chelsea Hotel where murder and death awaited him.

On 12 October 1978, Nancy Spungen was found dead in the bathroom of the couple's room on the first floor of the Chelsea Hotel, New York. She had bled to death from a single knife wound in her stomach. Sid Vicious was arrested at the hotel later that same day.

The news came as no surprise to avid Pistols watchers. The accident that had been waiting to happen had just happened. Just proof of what we all thought would be the outcome. Vicious had disintegrated what few brain cells he had left kicked in by the heroin. The incident was to seal the Pistols' notoriety for ever. Warners dropped Vicious and the other two quicker than EMI after Grundy-gate. Branson stood behind him, though, and, as a sign of their good faith in Sid's innocence, put up the bail for Vicious on 17 October, a cool $50,000.

McLaren claimed that Mick Jagger offered to stand bail, but this seemed a strange turn of events. Vicious and his pals were not Stones fans. McLaren would have bitten off Jagger's hand for the money. He told the *Melody Maker*, 'I did not like the idea of the record company paying up the bail because it then meant that you were basically in its control.'

McLaren could see the way the game was going and it was not even half-time. Lydon was cosying up to Branson as he was putting the finishing touches to his new band PiL. Vicious was fucked whichever way you looked at it, even if he did manage to walk on the murder charge. Jones and Cook were only pawns in the game of mind chess that was about to be played and even McLaren himself was very isolated now.

McLaren's brief, Steven Fisher, met Jagger at the Savoy Hotel for lunch to discuss his offer. For whatever reason, Jagger, in McLaren's words, 'hummed and hawed' about the matter. Jagger told him that the situation was complicated as Keith Richards was still awaiting trial on heroin charges in Toronto. The Mounties had busted old Keef and at that time he looked like he might be going down. For whatever reason, the money was not forthcoming. Actually, the whole mess was Keef's fault because he was a junkie in those days: Johnny Thunders tried to copy him, Vicious got into heroin because of Thunders…

McLaren flew to New York on 13 October to try to free his charge. It was rumoured that he approached the famous defence advocate F Lee Bailey, later one of OJ Simpson's defence lawyers, who had made his reputation arguing for a retrial for Dr Sam Sheppard, convicted of killing his wife but eventually found not guilty, and believed to be the inspiration for *The Fugitive* TV programme. Pictures of McLaren arriving in New York, wearing a tartan bondage suit similar to the one Lydon wore in San Antonio, show the strain and worry on his face. Cynics in London said that the manager wanted Vicious out on bail so as they could film his last few days of freedom. What an end to the *Swindle*. Even Russ Meyer could not have topped that one. If it had been made into a reality show, it would have made *The Osbournes* look like *The Good Life*.

McLaren seemed genuinely upset and concerned about Vicious. Their relationship, like Sid's with everyone in the world, had suffered as a result of his heroin habit and increasingly violent conduct. McLaren rallied round him nevertheless. Vicious's innocence will always be in doubt, and opinions will always conflict. Nick Kent wrote that Sid and Nancy should be 'left to rot'. Steve Jones's view was that she killed herself.

Columbo could have solved the crime for us easily. A pity he could not have answered the call to the Chelsea Hotel that autumn day. Friends of the couple in New York believed that Spungen's death was part of a double suicide pact of which Vicious backed out. In private, McLaren thought that Vicious had stabbed her in a row over drugs.

Vivienne Westwood, who had a great affection for Sid Vicious, also came round to that conclusion, but thought that Vicious never meant to kill his girlfriend. Whatever, far worse was to come, and what was left of McLaren's once powerful group would explode into a million pieces.

CHAPTER 14

RONNIE BIGGS

'Infamy! Infamy! They've all got it in for me!'
KENNETH WILLIAMS, CARRY ON CLEO

Ronnie Biggs was born on 8 August 1929 in Lambeth, South London. In 1947, at the age of 18, he joined the RAF, but two years later he was dishonourably discharged for desertion. Rather like McLaren's father, a life in the services did not hold any appeal for him. In 1963, he participated in the Great Train Robbery. The gang got away with an estimated £2.6m, an unthinkable amount in those days and the equivalent today of £40m plus. It was the most publicised crime in England of the 20th century.

During the course of the robbery, the train driver, Jack

Mills, was hit on the head with an iron bar. Biggs was tried and convicted of the robbery. The British establishment, furious at the scale and audacity of the robbery, handed out harsh sentences like sweets at a children's party. Ronnie and six others drew a 30-year slide, but in 1965 Biggs escaped from Wandsworth Prison by scaling the wall with a rope ladder. For the next 36 years, he was to live the life of a fugitive on the run. By 1978, after fleeing to Paris, Helsinki and eventually Australia, he was living openly in Rio de Janeiro. He couldn't be extradited from Brazil because local laws would not allow the father of a Brazilian child to be expelled. Biggs had fathered a child with his then girlfriend, Raimunda de Castro, a nightclub dancer.

One day he wrote a letter to an organisation in London called Glitterbest working out of an address at 90/98 Shaftesbury Avenue, London, very close to where Sandeman's Port were based.

In July 1978, Malcolm received a letter from 34 Rua Enngheiro Correa Nunes, Rio de Janeiro:

'Dear Malcolm. Thanks for your letter with the good tidings. But it is with some reluctance that I tie myself up with a pair of wankers like Jones and Cook. The promise of money finally persuaded me to throw in my lot with you and I can only hope that there will be no rip-offs or other forms of foul

*play. Don't forget I have a lot of mates in London.
Am standing by, ready for work or whatever – what
about a punk rock opus?'*

The letter went on about banking arrangements and a
request for copies of reviews of the record. It was signed
'RA Biggs the Great Train Robber'.

McLaren always claimed that his father Peter had
been a burglar. Perhaps the whole Biggs episode was his
first attempts at some reconciliation with his dad. When
Vicious and Lydon needed a father figure in their lives
in those crazy, turbulent months leading up to the
American trip, McLaren had been unable to respond.
He could not help because he did know how. To all
intents and purposes, Peter McLaren was a fugitive. He
could have been hiding out in South America or living
in South Australia.

As it happened, Peter McLaren never left England and
did not even possess a passport. According to the
records McLaren checked so thoroughly, Peter never
existed. Years later, McLaren traced him to a remote
part of Romney Marsh. Peter had a greasy spoon café
called The Oasis. Alan McGee would have approved.
McLaren was with CBS then, and they chauffeured him
and his brother Stewart to a meeting with their father.

It was a crazy place with art-deco petrol pumps from
a nearby 1930s garage, long since abandoned. McLaren

recalled that his father looked like WH Auden, weather-beaten, wearing white Levi's and a bright-green shirt. He had a German shepherd dog with him, and a shotgun. The meeting went OK, better than he could have expected, really. At one stage, Peter produced a picture of his mother Emily at 16, the same age Nancy Spungen was when she first started turning tricks and signing up for methadone cures. McLaren was surprised at how Jewish Emily looked, but also how beautiful…

Peter McLaren never achieved the fame of Ronnie Biggs. The Great Train Robbery was an inspiration for everything McLaren did to promote the Pistols, and it gave him a great deal of personal pleasure to act out a scam with Biggs. McLaren saw the Great Train Robbery as a political act committed against the establishment, which was why they reacted so strongly and punished so harshly. McLaren told the *Melody Maker*, 'It was not a crime in the sense of EMI being a crime. It was a fabulous anarchic attempt at destroying the status quo, very Robin Hood-ish and I suppose I still believe in all that. I'd live for doing that every day.

'The same humour was there with the Great Train Robbery as the *Today* show. The attempts by the police to track down the gang, the escape of Ronnie, then the public fury. The same fury that the public were to display when Steve Jones spoke to Bill Grundy.

'It's the only humour that you can laugh at. You

cannot laugh at Morecombe & Wise, can you? But you can imagine everybody reading about the Great Train Robbery and thinking, God, how fabulous.'

The Biggs jaunt grew from a germ of an idea McLaren had after the gig at Jack Ruby's old club in Dallas. Find Biggs, film a show in a club somewhere and then show it around the world. McLaren claimed that he told all of the Pistols of his idea. Jones and Cook were keen, but Vicious was reluctant because of his poor condition. Lydon claimed he only knew of the venture a few hours before the flight to Rio. Jones was adamant that he knew at least a week before. In any event, the band were booked on the 7am to Rio, but from there several versions of what happened next emerged.

It would appear that the band, without Sid, had a meeting in a Japanese hotel, the MiYako in San Francisco. Joe Stevens, a respected photographer, was covering the trip and witnessed the final break-up. He told Jon Savage about the meeting. 'John said to McLaren, "You're a miserable stupid cunt, you have been stitching me up ever since you met me. With the police, with people beating me up, robbing me, calling my house in the middle of the night, annoying me, telling lies about me to the press. And now you want me to sit on a plane with Sid Vicious for hours, you stupid cunt. To talk to some idiot who coshed somebody on a train."

'McLaren said, "You're turning into another fucking Rod Stewart, we do not need you, go and find some cocaine."'

That was about it really, end of an era. Vicious was in the hippie Haight-Ashbury district of town – where the original flower power, peace and love movement had flourished – bombed out of his head on smack. He later OD'd, then turned green on a plane on his way back to London. Booted off the plane, he ended up in the Jamaica Hospital in Queens, New York, before he got back to London and Nancy. Lydon was also in New York, with Joe Stevens. Eventually, only Jones and Cook flew down to Rio. They all had to get out of America quickly because they were only on a two-week visa.

McLaren went back to London to work on the film and set things up with Virgin about the Biggs deal. Jones and Cook stayed in Rio for nearly two months, getting on very well with Biggs. They were fans of each other, which always helps. Just a few years before, the film *Butch Cassidy and the Sundance Kid* had spawned the hit TV show *Alias Smith and Jones*. Both film and series featured a great deal of train robbing, which added kudos to the 20th-century version of a great train robbery. Butch and Sundance also had to take refuge in South America. Biggs, meanwhile, liked the idea of being a pop star, and in his letter to McLaren he enclosed a sample of his 'punk opus' that would have looked good on one of Vivienne's T-shirts. The obscenity laws forbid us from reproducing it here.

In their first meeting, Jones told Biggs about his early life on the thieve in White City, ducking and diving. Jones was a natural petty criminal, nothing safe in his presence. He told Biggs about when they used to steal stationery from Woolworths and sell it to their schoolmates. Woolworths, which didn't survive the credit crunch, no doubt would have been one of the first major outlets to refuse to stock 'God Save The Queen'. Steve Jones may have started their problems.

Jones went on to talk to Biggs about how he ended up in an 'approved school' (a type of prison for young offenders) for stealing cars. He also spent time in a remand home.

Steve Jones later had his own radio show in LA, *Jonesy's Jukebox*. For two hours every weekday, he played an eclectic bunch of records along with entertaining a varied selection of guests, including Sly Stone. One day McLaren rang the show to reminisce about the events leading up to the Biggs record.

'None of this would have happened without you,' McLaren said. 'You were the reason the Pistols were formed. You were the guy nicking the stuff out of my shop, driving me so bloody crazy I had to you give you a job. And then I had to help you form this group.

Ultimately, Steve, I would not have even thought about the Sex Pistols had it not been for you.'

Jones told *MOJO* magazine about the trip to Rio: 'We was not solid as a band and I just said, "I don't want to do this no more." My best thinking is to run. So that is what I did.

'It was a weird time. We had just broken up. Went to Brazil, me and Paul, and I thought it was great writing a track with Ronnie Biggs. I think that track ('No One Is Innocent') is great. Ronnie Biggs rated himself as a bit of a poet and I remember sitting in the hotel room writing the music while he wrote the words. It was a big accomplishment to write a song with an infamous train robber. That was a good move.'

It was a good move, McLaren's finest moment in many respects, the major McLaren contribution while the monster that the Sex Pistols had become was in its death throes. Lydon, snowbound in New York, Vicious on his eventual way to the Chelsea Hotel via drug hell, but the remaining Pistols were creating art with Biggsy. It could have been said to be his first true flourish as auteur. The single was called 'No One Is Innocent (A Punk Prayer By Ronnie Biggs)'. It was also known as 'Cosh The Driver', a provocative reference to the attack on the train driver Mills. It was never proved that Biggs had anything to do with the assault.

McLaren's idea was to show the idea that 'crime *did*

pay'. Biggs was the perfect example of a criminal leading a carefree existence in warm sunshine, thumbing his nose at the establishment. His other theme was more subtle. One of the song's verses is about Martin Bormann, a Nazi war criminal, who also hid out in South America. In the film, Bormann – actor James Jeter wearing a rubber mask – was supposed to have joined the Pistols' line-up. Combined, the two symbols were meant to alienate as much as 'God Save The Queen' did in 1977.

The crime rate in Britain was rising and law and order was seen as a major concern to the nation. The Nazi insignia and swastikas worn by the Bormann figure were the usual McLaren ploys, just as Siouxsie Sioux's armband had been. The war was still fresh in people's memories, and the symbols still potent in the minds of generations of people who had survived the war. Today, it would have just been banned. There was always a strong anti-Semitic undercurrent to a lot of McLaren's work. Caroline Coon picked up on it, and the reference to his mother's Jewishness when he saw Peter McLaren's picture of her was another clue. Sid Vicious had tongue-lashed Bernie Rhodes with racial abuse when he was on stage with Siouxsie at the 100 Club. The Holocaust references to Belsen and Auschwitz contained in Vicious's songs would not have been tolerated today.

McLaren also used it to offend the lefties and liberals

whom he despised as much as the racists themselves. In the late '70s, organisations like Rock Against Racism were emerging and McLaren was as anxious to upset them as much as he would *Guardian* readers.

The record was released in June 1978 and made the Top 10. The picture sleeve featured slides from the forthcoming film, later known as *The Great Rock'n'Roll Swindle*. The B-side was 'My Way', featuring Sid Vicious. This was turning out to be Vicious's finest moment as a Sex Pistol, specially recorded for *Swindle*. Sid hated the song and at first refused to sing it, but McLaren flattered his ego by suggesting that he change the lyric. No other artist would have the nerve. This idea appealed to Sid and he sat down and poured his heart out all about how Lydon had betrayed him.

Biggs never made anything much out of the success, however, and certainly not as much as he had hoped or expected. Al Clark of Virgin phoned up Biggs in Brazil and asked him if he would phone in some interviews to help promote the record. Biggs said he did not want to do any more unless he was paid for it, claiming that he'd done a deal with McLaren but as yet had not received any funds. Biggs asked Clark if he thought he was entitled to any royalties. Clark informed him that the record had done well and had reached the No 4 spot in the charts.

Biggs told him that he thought that, if a record made

the Top 5, he would automatically get a house and car. It was a wonderfully 1950s view of pop music, when the successful stars brought their grey-haired old mums nice suburban houses and Morris Minors. Clark told him not to expect a house and car, but he should get some money.

Biggs told him to bring the money over in a suitcase and when he got there he would have the 'best time of his life'. This may well have been true, but poor old Ronnie Biggs never made any money out of the single. Soon the company went into receivership and he never received his share. The great robber had been robbed by the biggest swindler in the business.

Sid Vicious, however, fared much worse: he lost his life. Bailed after Spungen's death, he was soon back in prison for smashing a broken bottle into the face of Patti Smith's brother, nearly blinding him. The incident happened in a New York disco after he had lewdly propositioned Smith's girlfriend, and Vicious was sent back to Rikers Island. The longer-term plan was to bail him again, then for him to go to Miami and record some tracks with his old chums Cook and Jones. It was rumoured that one of the tracks was going to be 'Mack the Knife'. (It was not known if 'First Cut is the Deepest', the Cat Stevens song that kept the Pistols off the top spot in Jubilee week, was another.) For a brief moment, hope flickered, with Nancy Spungen gone, perhaps they could clean up Sid and get him together. Vicious was still very maudlin, but touched that Cook and Jones had agreed to help him. Lydon was not involved.

McLaren's better spirits dipped when a hearing was set for a case brought against him by Lydon. McLaren was badly prepared for the case, still heavily involved with the film and Vicious's problems. Also, he lacked the temperament to think ahead. At one time, it looked like the whole sorry mess would be settled out of court but Lydon's legal team had decided on a receiver to be appointed. They could get a truer picture then of McLaren's Glitterbest company's finances. McLaren was confident that he would win the case.

Richard Branson claimed that he wanted a settlement that would allow both the Pistols and Lydon's new band, PiL, to co-exist on his label. Fat chance. Branson complained that McLaren's attitude to Lydon was 'stupid', while the Pistols' manager declared that Branson was in league with Lydon to bring him to court. Branson, he also claimed, was trying to make Lydon into a world star, and had sided with the singer to improve his 'public image' (pun intended) which would encourage younger hip bands to sign for Virgin.

McLaren's character in the *Swindle* film began to take him over. It was uncanny to watch. Warner Bros joined in the fun by suing McLaren for the film money. It was a sorry old time for him. Cash from Chaos. McLaren felt trapped.

Vicious was bailed again on 2 February 1979, almost two months after going back to Rikers. McLaren wanted to be there but was detained in London with his case in the High Court about to start. Once bail was arranged, Vicious left court with his mother to go to a celebration party held by his new girlfriend, Michelle Robinson. As soon as he arrived at the party, he injected some heroin his mother had bought for him, figuring that if he tried to score himself he would jeopardise his bail conditions. The next morning, Sid was found dead in the bedroom. While in Rikers, he had detoxified, which had possibly changed his tolerance level.

Rumours abounded: the heroin had been purer than he had expected, while another conspiracy theory suggested that it had been cut with strychnine. Suicide theories were also put forward, claiming he just couldn't face life without Nancy. Figures showed a high proportion of deaths from suicidal overdoses among non-therapeutic heroin addicts. Whatever, Sid took the mystery of Nancy's and his own death with him to the grave.

'He walked a tightrope all the time,' Vivienne Westwood said. 'Life and death. And it was not play acting. It was for real. We never had a chance to find out how good Sid would be with the right friends around him.'

McLaren was very distressed; he blamed himself. He had intended to go to New York to be with Vicious, but the pressures of the impending legal battle were weighing heavily on him. Maybe Vicious would have survived a little longer if McLaren had been around. He wanted Sid to go back to London to be buried on the basis that New York never did anything for him. Vicious himself once asked to be buried next to Nancy in Philadelphia, but even in death he was cheated of his wishes: his body was cremated in New York.

A few months later, McLaren received a sad little letter from Vicious's psychiatrist, Stephen S Teich. Part of it went as follows: 'It is hard to find words to express what I feel. I have just learned about Sid and I am searching my mind for what else I could have done. I, for one, feel you did as much as possible to help him in the way you knew. You acted beyond the formal role in your relationship. Clearly, he was someone you cared for.'

CHAPTER 15

WOW, IT'S BOW WOW WOW

*'Cunning and deceit will serve a man better than force
to rise from a base condition to great fortune.'*
NICCOLO MACHIAVELLI

*'The punk movement did not end with the demise of the
Pistols, but the head of the dragon was cut off.'*
MALCOLM MCLAREN

The hearing between McLaren and Lydon began on 7 February 1979 in Court 37 of the Chancery Law Courts in the Strand. It lasted for a fortnight, finishing just days before the soundtrack for *The Great Rock'n'Roll Swindle* was released, sans Lydon. The film was still being edited but it was a mess. Lydon came to the court every day, sometimes wearing the blue and red check Zoot suit he had worn on stage in America. It went well with the mauve creepers. McLaren sat on the other side of the room wearing a large black fake-fur coat, but they never acknowledged one another, never even looked at each other. The last time they had spoken was the night in the hotel when they argued about the Biggs trip.

Lydon was fighting McLaren for the Pistols heritage, against Ronnie Biggs, Swastikas and Belsen references. Lydon was not McLaren's pet monkey, even if McLaren was treating him like one, a working-class prop that he discarded when he did not require him any more. (When PiL's *First Issue* was released in December 1978 to mediocre reviews, and his Christmas Day concerts at the Rainbow received similar lukewarm responses, some cynics suggested that he needed a manager.)

Lydon had hired some blue-chip players – though his QC, John Wilmer, was to die of cancer shortly after the case, he was brilliant during the trial. He painted McLaren as a Svengali figure totally influencing the four young Pistols. Lydon said that he did not understand the five-year agreement he had signed in the autumn of 1976, but thought that it had given McLaren too much control.

The major issue, however, was the film. It was estimated that, between September 1976 and March 1978, Glitterbest had made just under half-a-million pounds. Rather than pay these royalties to the band, they were redirected to the film. All that was left was nearly £30,000.

The official receiver asked McLaren to assist with the film but he was sickened by the idea of working for them. Disgusted by the events, he did not even attend an important meeting with them. Instead, he flew to France and self-imposed exile on the continent. McLaren was heartbroken, his manager-ship frozen. Even Jones and Cook, always staunch McLaren supporters, had defected to the other side.

McLaren headed for Paris, like Napoleon on the way back from Moscow. He was broke and left behind him debts in the region of £50,000. Jamie Reid told *NME* that McLaren 'had been stabbed in the back'. The court case had been a victory for Virgin.

McLaren, meanwhile, told the *NME*, 'It was a strange period. It helped me get some perspective on England, everything looked much smaller.' With some new acquaintances he ended up making three porno films. He was working for 'these guys from Marseilles'. He went on to say, 'I had never done a job before when someone said, "Do this, do that, here's your wages." I was quite chuffed.'

McLaren took some time off to roam around Southern Europe, soaking up the sun, sea and whatever. For the first time in years, he was a free spirit. Eventually, he was pulled back to London by the prospect of a TV series for Granada Television called *An Insider's Guide to the World of the Music Business*. McLaren had some great new ideas for the series, seeing it as an effective means of promoting new artists and showcasing their record. Simon Cowell does the same thing today in a more mainstream method, but McLaren's methods were, in his words, 'too over the top for them'. Sadly, the series was never made, and once again McLaren found himself in limbo.

In October 1979, McLaren and Westwood were attending a wedding reception at the Portobello Hotel. It was an old haunt of his and he had worked there on the original script for *Who Killed Bambi?*. Stuart Goddard, there with Jordan, approached him. McLaren, remembering Goddard from when he had sung with Bazooka Joe, asked how his band was doing. The would-be Adam Ant was trying to get his career moving forward after various setbacks and band personnel changes, and was being managed by Jordan. For almost three hours, McLaren lectured him on the music business, probably the same rap he would have included in the ill-fated *Insider's Guide...* show. McLaren had seen the future, and it was 'videodiscs'. The actual discs never took off but he was correct in realising that the pop video was the future, still is.

McLaren knew that whoever made the best video was going to rule the world and for a while Stuart, in his alter ego of Adam Ant, did. Emerging from the first wave of punk, Adam became the first real superstar of the '80s. He was clever; he borrowed McLaren's ideas and, with the Bowie-esque ability to change, gave the world the look of the dandy highwayman. When

McLaren had returned from Paris, he found that Westwood was up to her ears in her new look of ruffles and pirate clothes. Among the advice McLaren had handed Adam Ant was to 'Take the white stripe of Geronimo, take the tribal beat of ethnic music. Be a pirate – plunder the world's music.'

There's a case to make that the global success of Johnny Depp's *Pirates of the Caribbean* films could be linked with Adam Ant sowing the pirate image into the MTV generation's consciousness, just as McLaren's impressionable childhood was influenced through reading about the exploits of Blackbeard and Captain Blood. Of course, Keith Richards, when not influencing other impressionable youths like Johnny Thunders and Nick Kent, was also doing his bit for the pirate look by transforming himself from the beautiful young man he was in the days of Andrew Loog Oldham to the cut-throat, junkie look of later years.

Adam learned so well that his paint-streaked cheekbones, second only to Siouxsie's in the punk beauty list, curling lipsticked mouth, pigtails, ruffles and ribbons changed the look of the '80s high street in the same way that safety pins and ripped T-shirts had in the previous decade. It made him the figurehead of the movement that again caught the mood and flavour of the times. The ex-Bazooka Joe singer went on to hobnob with another dandy highwayman called Michael

Jackson. As he tried to crash into Hollywood, he hung around with Liza Minnelli. But the wheel spun and Adam Ant had bad times: on the comeback trail, he still goes in 430 King's Road asking for discount on Vivienne's stock.

This was all to come, however, and at first McLaren managed him. One day he gave him a tape of tracks he should listen to. It included: 'Mystery Train', Elvis Presley; 'YMCA', Village People; 'Got To Pick A Pocket Or Two!', Ron Moody (from the *Oliver!* soundtrack); 'Hot Dog', Taps Miller; 'Hello! I'm Back Again', Gary Glitter; and 'Burundi Black', Burundi Black.

The last track was particularly interesting. Adam had never heard anything like it before. McLaren had discovered it while sitting in a music library in Paris one day trying to find pieces of classical music with expired copyright for the soundtrack of his friend's porn movies. The sound captivated him, as we are to see.

Adam brought the Burundi drum sound into vogue when he used it on his string of hits 'Dog Eat Dog', 'Stand and Deliver' and 'Kings of the Wild Frontier'. Not only did he have the sound to make hits, but he had the best videos with the prettiest girls and the best costumes. The vision he displayed in the uncharted field of pop video helped define the MTV era.

A point could be made here – at this time, John Lydon was also well-placed to make a similar leap into global stardom. He had, after all, beaten McLaren in court and had the backing of the Virgin publicity machine. But he lacked the commercial appeal and the chocolate box good looks of an Ant. The death of Lydon's boyhood friend Sid had been a reminder of the massive price tag that came with huge success and must also have sapped his motivation.

Adam Ant had that glamour in bundles, but by now McLaren was no longer managing him, having decided to dump the singer from the band. The wisdom of this in hindsight points to another 'glorious failure' by McLaren but that was his game plan, always was. McLaren told *NME*, 'The first thing to do was dump Adam.'

In his autobiography Adam Ant states that, 'After weeks of indoctrination and ego building by Malcolm the Ants had ceased to be.' Perhaps Malcolm did not consider Adam to be of sufficient star quality to front a world-famous band. In a strange way he thought Adam was too old for his new ideas. He told *NME*, 'Any kid of 18 I met was so self-conscious they could not relax and be themselves. That what was so great about Annabella [Lwin], she had the confidence to be herself. I think that age group [13-14 year olds] have the ability not to give a damn. They believe themselves to be intelligent and they have a confidence about themselves.'

Jamie Reid, still loyal to his old art-school friend, sat in with McLaren for the endless mind-numbing hours of auditions looking for a replacement. The wannabes were all mini Lydons or the new kid on the block Jimmy Pursey. If they made a film of all this, Danny Dyer would get the role of Pursey. He had his eyes on the crown now, fusing the elements of punk and football hooliganism. His shows were a mixture of *The Firm* and some of Julien Temple's footage of the Pistols playing on the boat trip.

McLaren was on the point of quitting and going back to Europe, the taste to wander strong. Then one day he walked into his local laundrette and discovered Annabella. The 14-year-old was to cause, in her own way, as big a stir as the Pistols had. It was like a moment out of a Hollywood musical. McLaren heard her singing a song from Stevie Wonder's *Songs in the Key of Life* and that was it. Born of Burmese parentage, Lwin had been in England for six years. Like McLaren she had a stepfather, a Greek man whom McLaren had a difficult job convincing about his plans for his stepdaughter. Lwin had spent most of her time in England with her aunt in Devon and had been trying to drop out of school for some time. Eventually, she went to the audition wearing her mother's ill-fitting clothes. The rest of the band were shocked at the time but they soon warmed to her sparkling personality and were wowed by her singing. The 'wow' factor was coming into play because McLaren changed the name of the remnants of Adam's backing band to Bow Wow Wow.

It was not an easy start for Lwin. She was thrown out of the band three times for various problems and early live appearances did not draw great reviews. (Let us not forget, though, that the Pistols only had one person clapping at the end of their first show.) McLaren had the belief, however, and even invested some of the money he had made in France in making a tape and hawking it around the record companies.

Their first single, released on EMI, was 'C30, C60, C90 Go'. It was a pro-piracy (that word again) song and concern was expressed at high levels in the music business that a single was put out promoting the advantages of home taping. McLaren was foretelling the future once again: even if the demise of the business has not been down to home taping, it was the start of the rot. The record company issued the single as a C10 cassette, selling at the same price as the single (about £1.10). Some of the cassettes came in a mock tin of Bow Wow Wow dog food and are now about as rare as the A&M Pistols 'God Save The Queen' single.

An artefact from another lost Empire but it still sounds good, three minutes of mock Burundi drumming, a slice of '77 buzz-saw guitar and Lwin's hard-edged vocal, sounding like Janis Joplin on speed. McLaren got a credit for the song along with Barbe/Ashman/Gorman and it made the Top 40. McLaren was pleased with it and with her new look: with encouragement from the band, she shaved her beautiful black hair above the ears and kept pigtails. Within six months the look had caught on as kids everywhere copied it. McLaren told the *Sunday Mirror*, 'She has turned the shaven head into something extremely sensual.'

Annabella's mother, Mrs Aimee Dun-Lwin, was in a state of shock at the transformation. Once again the old Svengali charges were levied against him.

'She threatened to sue me' McLaren said in the same *Sunday Mirror* interview. 'She said I changed her daughter, poisoned her mind and altered her mind to something she can no longer talk or relate to. It may even be true, but I think Annabella's a lot better for it.

'I am sure her mother would have liked to kill me. She tried to get a court order to keep Annabella from working outside her jurisdiction.'

The album *Your Cassette Pet* followed, but by now EMI were refusing to promote the band, who they deemed a menace to the industry through advocating home taping, and in May 1981 McLaren signed Bow Wow Wow to RCA. At one time, he had gone for a job there but had horrified his selection panel by calling one of their biggest stars, Dolly Parton, a 'cunt' and suggesting to them that they drop her from the label as unceremoniously as he had axed Adam Ant.

A further hit followed with 'Go Wild in the Country' (No 7 in the UK) and yet another controversy because young Annabella appeared to be naked on the cover. It was the most controversial sleeve since Jamie Reid's 'God Save The Queen', but this time it was a take on Manet's *Le Dejeuner sur L'herbe* (The Luncheon on the Grass).

A remake of The Strangeloves hit 'I Want Candy' gave them another Top 10 chart placing in 1982. McLaren was getting restless, though, and was keen to add another singer to the line-up to give it another dimension. And a chap from another dimension joined briefly, one George O'Dowd, soon to shake up the world in his alter ego of Boy George. BBC ran a series of plays about the '80s in the early summer of 2010, shortly after McLaren's death. One of the plays was about Boy George, featuring Malcolm McLaren as a *Carry On*-type character, a mixture of Kenneth Williams and Charles Hawtrey, living in an mansion with Jamie Reid artwork and bricks flying through the window.

McLaren had invented a character called Lieutenant Lush and he wanted George to adopt this personae. Who the Lush character was based on was never explained, but eventually George was booted out, just like Adam Ant. Same story: the 'boy' went on to be probably the biggest name of his era followed by the usual drugs, fall from grace tabloids routine. George O'Dowd even ended up sweeping the streets he used to own while serving a community sentence.

McLaren was always of the view that Bow Wow Wow

could have made it as big in America as Boy George and Adam Ant were. In his interview with Nick Momus, he explained, 'They were on the cusp and could easily have been a big group in the United States. They needed that third album; it's always the third album.

'I left after the second album. I wanted to make my own record at the time. I was not frankly interested in pursuing them. But I did genuinely think if they got a manager and they were able by then to write their own songs... Because I wrote 95 per cent of the lyrics and I think by then they were ready to write their own. I can honestly say they would have survived. The Sex Pistols were never going to survive.'

In his tribute programme on BBC, Lwin was interviewed. Now in her forties but still sparkling and attractive, she blamed the failure of the band to reach global status on McLaren, 'the spoiled child'. He walked away when he did not get his own way.

McLaren's next venture was his most successful post-Pistols project. He launched the World's Famous Supreme Team, a modestly named hip-hop crew he saw playing a black party in New York with Afrika Bambaataa. They combined traditional American folk music with the new styles of hip hop and scratching, and the Top 10 single 'Buffalo Gals' was born.

McLaren was working with the producer Trevor Horn, of Frankie Goes to Hollywood fame. Horn had the chance of working with Spandau Ballet on their latest album but he was so impressed with McLaren he decided that it might be more fun. It certainly sounded it. Horn found an old square-dancing song, McLaren had been to Johannesburg with him and they had recorded some stuff with some Zulu women. They had been highly amused by the fact that McLaren could not sing, a fact that he did not conceal and never had. (He did contribute to *The Great Rock'n'Roll Swindle* soundtrack with his unique version of 'You Need Hands'.) McLaren did some rapping on the record, Horn mixed it all up and the rest was history.

The emergence of McLaren as a pop star was another swindle of the record business. As the Zulu lady said, he could not sing, he could not dance, he was not young or good looking, but he could always concoct a fantasy. The records flowed like wine, some of it fine, others not so much. One gem, though, was a version of 'Madam Butterfly' that made the Top 20 in 1984. It also topped the Italian charts for three months, a country that knows a thing or two about opera. An album called *Fans* followed, plundering the story lines of *Carmen* and *Turandot*, with an amazing accompanying video packed with the top models of the day.

Torn between fashion and music, his relationship with Vivienne Westwood finally ended and McLaren headed for Hollywood in the hopes of becoming a movie producer. His agenda was to translate his entrepreneurial skills into movies. A chance encounter with Steven Spielberg led to him being put on the payroll; Spielberg had loved the 'Madam Butterfly' record, which opened the door for him. For the next few years, he would spend eight hours a day bashing out possible movie plots.

While out there he had an intense affair with Lauren Hutton, film star and model. That was when he met Orson Welles, who advised him to return home or risk ending up like him. McLaren was becoming more and more saddened by the whole process and, taking Welles's advice, he quit Hollywood. Instead of England, however, McLaren again headed for Paris where he made another album about the city he loved. This featured two of the most beautiful women the city had known: Catherine Deneuve and Françoise Hardy.

Eventually, the wanderer returned to London and decided to run for mayor. Alan McGee, who had used a lot of McLaren-esque tactics to promote his own world-famous band Oasis, bankrolled him. How serious 'Citizen McLaren' was remained to be seen, but he certainly livened it up. He later pulled out of the race, as he did from *I'm A Celebrity, Get Me Out Of Here*. His health was not good, but he kept it to himself.

CHAPTER 16

THE FUNERAL (TOO FAST TO LIVE, TOO YOUNG TO DIE)

'What are they gonna say when's he gone?
That he was a kind man, that he was a wise man,
he had plans, he had wisdom. Bullshit.'
Photojournalist (Dennis Hopper) on Colonel Kurtz
(Marlon Brandon), *Apocalypse Now*

'Trust Malcolm McLaren to be late for his own funeral,' the old punk bellowed. It was 1.45pm on 22 April 2010. A beautiful spring afternoon and the bright sunshine had caught most people unawares after the most brutal winter for decades, well since McLaren first strutted down the King's Road in that blue suit.

The punk must have been about 50, with dreadlocks and a faded yellow T-shirt with something stencilled on it about 'Anarchy'. He was wearing the obligatory tartan trousers and a heavy, bible-black jacket that was studded on the shoulders, the sun glinted on the piercing on his face. Doc Martens completed the outfit, incongruous on such a hot day.

The press had advertised that the cortège was passing through Camden High Street at 1.15pm before meandering down Chalk Farm Road, Ferdinand Street, Malden Road and Southampton Road, before ending up at Highgate Cemetery. Even though Camden has been cleaned up as a tourist attraction, it still had enough sleaze to make it comfortable for McLaren's last ride.

It was hard to determine exactly how many people were there to pay their humble respects to the former mayoral candidate. The beautiful weather had attracted many tourists to Camden anyway, plus, being lunchtime, there were many office and shop workers on their break. There must have been hundreds of fans, though, who had come expressly to say goodbye to the godfather of punk rock.

Another punk joined the dreadlocked one. His hair, like the economy, was in deep recession. What was left of it, though, was dyed purple. He was insistent that there must have been another tribute going on for McLaren, probably in close proximity to the shop in the King's Road.

'They wouldn't let it pass without a celebration, hope we haven't missed a trick coming up here.'

The white Rastafarian nodded sagely.

One of Malcolm McLaren's favourite movies was *House of Games* with the line: 'A sucker born every minute, huh?' 'And two to take him!'

Earlier, the private funeral service had taken place at the deconsecrated One Marylebone Church opposite Great Portland Street Station, just north of his old playground Oxford Street. The guests included Vivienne Westwood, sporting a headband that said 'Chaos'. In the sunlight her orange hair looked even brighter and her skin even more ghostly white, rather like a scene from *Interview with the Vampire*.

Two of the four surviving Pistols sat together, Glen Matlock wearing a striped jacket with a velvet collar and Paul Cook in a sharp shiny suit and crisp shirt and tinted glasses. He had made the effort. Cook sang along to McLaren's version of Max Bygraves's 'You Need Hands' from the *Swindle* soundtrack, which prompted dancing in the aisles from some of the congregation, a punk wearing an armband bearing a knuckleduster and scissor motif pogoing with a blonde in a vinyl mini-skirt.

John Lydon was touring America with a reconstructed PiL: strangely enough, the night after the funeral, the group's concert in Tucson was abandoned due to bad weather. Interesting to speculate if he would have attended the funeral. Lydon's comments at the time of McLaren's death – 'Malc was always entertaining and I hope you remember that. Above all else he was an entertainer and I will miss him' – contrasted sharply with those he made in an interview with *Record Collector* magazine in 2005: 'The man never helped me none. He never made my life comfortable. I have taken severe hidings and knifings while he ran and hid. He never helped us out. He never kept us together as a band. He never even kept us together as friends.'

The situation between the two was never resolved in McLaren's lifetime, only death cured the bad blood that flowed between them.

Other luminaries among the congregation were Sir Bob Geldof and Tracey Emin, wearing some strange-looking footwear, a copy of the shoes worn by Dorothy in Oz. Geldof had been a rival of McLaren's when he had fronted his own band The Boomtown Rats in the late '70s. The Rats had the first new-wave No 1, but his work in setting up Band Aid had considerably changed his profile and that day he looked eminently respectable in a dark suit and RayBans, so different from the guy that was seriously out there in those days.

The mourner that drew the most attention in the media, though, was Adam Ant. His appearance caused a stir even in such an assortment of styles and fashions. Stuart Leslie Goddard was wearing an eye-popping chalk-striped suit with bondage trousers and a trilby hat. In the hatband, he had placed torn-out photographs of himself in his heyday with chiselled features and pirate regalia. Another photograph depicted McLaren circa 1978. Reminders of better times, before Adam became lost. What was once a glittering career lay in tatters, having bottomed out in 2003 when he was arrested and sectioned under the Mental Health Act.

As always, the rumour mill was working overtime, pumping out news on Adam Ant. He had been recording in Moscow (which might explain the Moscow State Circus flyer tucked next to McLaren's photograph) with Andy Bell of Oasis and former Ant Marco Pirroni. The new album had the surreal title of *Adam Ant Is The Blueblack Hussar in Marrying The Gunner's Daughter*. It included a tribute to his one-time mentor McLaren called 'Who's A Goofy Bunny Then?'. The song, originally conceived in the '80s, was a reference to McLaren's buck teeth, always a source of amusement to Adam.

At the start of the service Adam pointed towards the coffin where at the time a little girl was tap dancing next to it, and announced, 'He was Danton, Robespierre and the French Revolution all rolled into one. He was the Terror. He was a fucking hand grenade.'

Possibly Adam Ant was getting a tad confused with McLaren's interest with the Situationist movement and its founding member Guy Debord, which was a little after the French Revolution.

The McLaren family had put out a call for fans throughout the land to celebrate his life with 'one minute of mayhem', playing extremely loud music or doing something outrageous. Some metaphor of his life as an offence against the present-day culture.

A motley collection of punks had assembled outside Camden tube station, mellowed by Special Brew, although it was early. One of them had a CD and they put on the 1979 Sex Pistols version of 'My Way'. Sid's hoarse and croaking version was at first dismissed as just another salvo in the eternal war between punk and middle-of-the road schlock. However, like most of what McLaren did, it was no simple exercise in mockery.

'My Way' was a French chanson before Paul Anka changed the lyrics. It became Sinatra's most famous song through the power of his interpretation and the fact that he stamped his personality on it. Yet it fitted both the colourful life of Malcolm McLaren and the short tragedy of Vicious's perfectly. With his covert tribute to the song, McLaren, as with so many other things, led the pack. Both Sinatra and McLaren's careers had their ups and downs or, as he put it, 'glorious failures'. The song, however, was an attestation of affinities between the father of punk and a man whose tempestuous career made him the role model singer of the 20th century.

Eventually, the motorcade reached Camden High Street. The police had switched off the traffic lights and provided an escort. Two Daimler limos headed the procession, and there was also a green-painted London bus packed with mourners. Its destination? 'Nowhere', the same word that featured on the bus depicted on the cover of 'Pretty Vacant'. A further bus appeared on the cover bearing the word 'Boredom', artwork courtesy of Jamie Reid.

Just outside Camden Town underground station, the bus, moving as slow as ketchup, was halted by the crowd, opposite a shop called American Apparel. 'Buffalo Gals' was blaring at full volume, and we all knew 'Anarchy' would automatically follow.

Then came the carriage that carried McLaren's coffin, a small card indicating that the funeral company was Leverton & Sons. The coffin was matt black, but sprayed on the side was the slogan, 'Too fast to live, too young to die', the one-time name of McLaren's King's Road shop. Pulling the carriage were four black horses with plumes on their elegant heads. A huge floral tribute spelling out 'CASH FROM CHAOS' was there inside the carriage.

That was the buzzword that day: Chaos and Cash. Joe Corre had created a special T-shirt with that logo emblazoned across it to commemorate his father's passing. A mere £45 with the proceeds going towards his human rights charity Humanade. It was almost in the fashion of the 'Frankie Says Relax' T-shirt popularised by Frankie Goes to Hollywood in the '80s, a slogan Paul Morley had coined at the height of the band's popularity as he strove to promote them in a manner not seen since McLaren had fired the Pistols at the heart of England's establishment. As the procession went through Camden, Eddie Tudor-Pole, formerly of Tenpole Tudor, the man who had replaced Rotten in the Sex Pistols, was throwing bits of paper from the bus down into the crowd. At first there was a rush as the punks thought it might have been real cash, but when they finally fluttered down to the pavement it turned out to be flyers advising the £45 T-shirts.

Two nights later, BBC2 showed a tribute to the inspirational manager entitled *Malcolm McLaren – Artful Dodger*. It seemed that even in death the Dickensian shtick still followed McLaren. (Dickens' younger brother Alfred was buried in Highgate Cemetery, along with their parents John and Elizabeth.) The programme was produced by Alan Yentob, creative director of the BBC, who also attended the funeral. Yentob, who had a Jewish background, had become friends with McLaren in the '80s. The BBC man had cut his teeth on pop documentaries and was responsible for the David Bowie masterpiece *Cracked Actor* in the '70s.

Among the excellent footage shown was the clip from *The Great Rock'n'Roll Swindle* of McLaren wearing the 'Chaos' T-shirt and chucking clippings about the Pistols on to the fire. Another high spot was McLaren on a boat going down the Thames, recounting a similar journey years before. He had adopted the prissy tone and personae of 'The Embezzler' again.

Paul Morley was also on the show, lavishing on this seeming anachronism a respect bordering on – or amounting to – veneration. But it wasn't just talking heads like Morley who were shoring up McLaren's position in our daily lives. On the morning of the funeral, veteran DJ Sarah Kennedy played 'Buffalo Gals' on her early-morning Radio 2 show. On a playlist that usually included vapid spots for show tunes and big-band swing-time records, it sounded wilfully abstract.

The cortège arrived at Highgate Cemetery, the last resting place of Malcolm McLaren, and it seemed a fitting burial ground for him. McLaren had instructed that he be buried there because the cemetery had featured in *Swindle*. Packed with trees, bushes, shrubs and wild flowers and known for its wild life, it was opened in 1839 and housed a glut of Gothic tombs and mausoleums. With the current vogue for all things vampire, it could not have been more fashionable. Some might say McLaren was a cultural vampire, sucking the life blood out of anything that interested him.

Other famous occupants of the cemetery include Karl Marx, the father of Communism, and another well-known Russian, Alexander Litvinenko. Litvinenko, in best McLaren fashion, was a dissident and stern critic of modern-day Russia who had been poisoned.

A platoon of punks had caught the tube to Archway from Camden and walked in the warm sun up the hill to the cemetery. A curt notice awaited them stating that it was a private funeral and the gates were locked. Some young punks tried to clamber over the wall but they were discouraged from doing so by patrolling police officers. One of the punks had a passing resemblance to a young Sid Vicious before the drugs had ravaged his appearance. They waited by the gates sipping from cans of lager.

After about an hour, the ceremony was finished, ending with Westwood throwing a wreath on top of the coffin. The headstone bore the double M logo with 'McLaren was here' beneath. A huge sheet with the same wording was hung from the back of the bus. The limos drove away at high speed. At the gates there were still about 100 people, with an air of festivity, adrenaline, a buzz.

His partner Young Kim was in the last car. Westwood was in the first limo, Adam Ant in another. The 'Nowhere' bus was last to leave and the young Sid punk jumped on the back. The driver of the bus stopped the vehicle and jumped out, looking like he'd escaped from the set of *Mad Max 2* with a leather waistcoat and dark spiky hair, weighed down with chains and wearing knee-high 'pig-stomping' boots. The Federales waved the punk away.

'Boys will be boys.' Perhaps McLaren was thinking the same thing.

CHAPTER 17

MALCOLM MCLAREN'S HERITAGE

'Punk is now part of English heritage.'
MALCOLM MCLAREN

*'He was a visionary and took what was going on in
New York City and made it global. He was a massive
influence on everyone whoever had a punk shop or a punk
band. His passing represented the final chapter in an era
when music was exciting.'*
SYLVAIN SYLVAIN, NEW YORK DOLLS

A nice tribute from Sylvain – who said at the time of
McLaren's death that he was still waiting for his
friend to send him the ticket for a flight to London and
the job with the Sex Pistols. Sylvain was back in London
that summer playing some shows with former New York
Dolls singer David Johansen

Johansen was also fulsome in his praise for his former boss. 'McLaren was such a marvellous amalgam of exuberation, sensuality, culture and literacy.'

That legacy he left us is everywhere. The author saw a young Afro-Caribbean girl in a brown school uniform on the first really hot day of the summer of 2010 as London baked in a rare heat. Over it she wore a long white shirt covered in slogans and names. One of them read 'I am no Nigga'. The author wanted to ask her the meaning of it all but did not pursue the matter. McLaren had given a directive before to the school kids to cut up their blazers and deface them and it was good to see his ideas being carried out.

On the same day, Tracey Emin appeared in the *Evening Standard* colour magazine when she attended a butterfly-themed party wearing a costume designed by Vivienne Westwood. The same paper had recently featured Ralph Lauren denim artfully faded and torn – at a mere £1,140. Punk lived on, the puppet master would have approved of that one. Who said the future tells us what the past is about?

House of Fraser at Croydon that evening had in its fashion department a range of clothes by Diesel entitled '1978', the year that McLaren masterminded the Pistols' American tour. The outfit copied the nylon bomber-style jacket Lydon had worn in Atlanta the night he asked the audience, 'Aren't we the worst thing you have ever seen?' Underneath the latest version, there was a copy of a T-shirt with safety pins in it.

Further down the road another department store, Alders, had a new range of retro rock T-shirts. One had a young male model dressed as Sid Vicious in a black leather jacket, like the NYPD mug shots that were taken in 1978 when he was charged with killing Nancy Spungen, and while McLaren was trying to hustle the bail money. Not as controversial as the one Vivienne Westwood rushed out in Seditionaries when she heard the news: 'She is dead – I am alive'. When quizzed by the press about the taste of the garment, she said, 'I care more about Sid than Nancy. I was also aware that some people would think that it was a bit sick and I did it for that reason, because I like to upset people.'

Across the road in HMV, you could buy a DVD of Alex Cox's *Sid And Nancy* biopic, now partly rehabilitated by punk historians. In his autobiography, Lydon dismissed it as: 'Someone else's fucking fantasy, some graduate who missed the punk era. The bastard.'

Apart from *The Great Rock'n'Roll Swindle* and *The Filth and the Fury* DVDs available, you could buy some punk badges. They included the usual suspects, Jamie Reid's 'God Save The Queen' and the cover of 'Never Mind...' Symbols of the time that McLaren tweaked the establishment's nose till it squealed, the cultural virus was now mainstream.

The latest CD by hip-hop group Cypress Hill was also on sale, their first record in six years. It included a sample of 'Buffalo Gals' that was a posthumous tribute McLaren would have relished. The influence of that record could not be underestimated. McLaren's partner Young Kim stated on his BBC2 tribute show, 'He was being sued by his record company about it as they were not pleased with it.' Marvin Gaye had the same problem with Motown when he handed in *What's Going On*.

In an interview with Gavin Martin of *NME* at the time Charisma Records released 'Buffalo Gals', McLaren displayed just how far advanced his thinking was. It also showed how the music press of the day had misjudged him. (McLaren had sold Bow Wow Wow on the idea of looking good and feeling rich; George Michael had harnessed this into Wham! and grabbed the pubescent market that McLaren had sought.)

'I am an artist, I am,' he said. 'I always was and always will be. I think the reason Bow Wow Wow did not become popular was because Annabella was not me. She basically did not come from the street, she came from the laundrette. Eventually, I decided it was easier to walk down the road myself.

'This record ['Buffalo Gals'] showed that the world is getting smaller. England is closer to El Salvador than it is to West Germany. We don't own anything here but what we have is the ability to become the first modern nomads. We will make the changes that affect the rest of the world.'

Very accurately, the *NME* now saw the cunning manipulator as a self-indulgent, arty type playing little games for his own sake. Chastened by experience, McLaren was still taking risks; he went to Johannesburg during apartheid. McLaren also ventured into the Bronx looking for gems in dangerous places. He told *Swindle* magazine, 'It was around 1980. I was managing Bow Wow Wow and they were playing a showcase gig for RCA. I had never been further than 62nd Street and had always wondered what was further up. So I decided to take a walk. I saw a humongous guy on the streets of Harlem wearing a Sex Pistols T-shirt. His name was Afrika Bambaataa.'

One of McLaren's most memorable quotes was: 'I never think till I open my mouth, that makes things far more interesting.' Possibly that is why his movie projects didn't always make it to the multiplex screens. *Vanity Fair* had given him a big spread thanks to the silver-tongued McLaren's masterpiece of media hustling, but the filmmakers were always nervous. In *Sunset Boulevard*, the disillusioned screenwriter Gillis tells Norma Desmond, 'Last one I wrote was about Okies in the Dust Bowl. You would never know because, when it reached the screen, the whole thing played on a torpedo boat.'

McLaren had so many ideas for films, a riveting one was the *Rock'n'Roll Godfather*, a gangster-style musical he planned for almost a decade. It was about the late Peter Grant, who McLaren recalled from his Soho coffee bar days, the manager and 'fifth' member of Led Zeppelin. A tough negotiator, Grant flew Zeppelin to the stars. McLaren described the film to *The Sunday Times*: 'It is the story of how the rock business grew from its gangster-ish origins into a corporate monster through the efforts of one massive man.'

Massive was the key word here. Weighing in at 300lb and 6'5" tall, Grant was a giant in every sense of the word, particularly in his appetites for cocaine and heroin. With £20m earmarked for the project, Liam Neeson was approached for the lead role. The problem was, although they were keen and the Hollywood backers were anxious to exploit the nostalgia of the time, they were concerned about the power of the Led Zeppelin organisation, which was reluctant to release any music for the film. Grant's family were also worried about what McLaren's script would do to Peter's reputation.

With McLaren in the cab of the locomotive there would have been no stopping the express, but in the end the film never got made. The success of subsequent British gangster films like Guy Ritchie's *Lock, Stock and Two Smoking Barrels* and the Danny Dyer franchise showed the market available for British gangster films. Add to that the music angle and you had another potential *Performance* in the making.

McLaren's insistence that he was an artist was supported by one of England's greatest artists, Peter Blake. His former teacher told *The Sunday Times* in the '80s when the Royal Academy contemplated holding an exhibition based on McLaren's career, 'He is an artist. He has achieved marvellous collage techniques in his *Duck Rock* album, a pick'n'mix of African and western music. The Sex Pistols are not all what he is about. They were a contrived affair.'

McLaren took up the idea. 'It's ridiculous to say punk has nothing to do with art. The people I took up with were living sculptures. Punk is now part of the English heritage.

'People buy a heritage of either the changing of the guard or a punk. Nobody in the art world likes the idea of the artist who does not use a brush. I am an artist without portfolio. My career has been a brilliant act which is art and deserves to be seen as art.'

John Lydon would argue about the Pistols being contrived. In an interview with *Record Collector*, he talked about those beleaguered times. 'He started to believe his own Svengali nonsense. It was a good mind game, and we used to get on all right with each other until he started to believe all that as a genuine form of existence – and it is not. He always tends to copy someone, he did with Andy Warhol. I am a living monument… all preposterous, and it's been done better. He was always jealous of me. Because he wanted the credit.'

Lydon tried to convey the reference to Andy Warhol, documenting the human *mise-en-scene* in his silver-lined factory, as another putdown, but over the years it has come back to haunt him. He always contested the notion of McLaren as the creator of the Pistols, calling him an 'egomaniac traitor'. McLaren always called Lydon a 'collaborator' with the despised music business.

When the Pistols first re-formed in 1996, McLaren made these amusing comments to *The Independent*: 'I wish I cared more. I try to but I can't. I suppose it's because it's antique, it's in a vacuum, it's in a frame. It's part of a compilation of oldies. If you think about it, is it really any different from a Gerry and the Pacemakers reunion?'

What was the root cause of their problem though? Christakis Charalambous was a McLaren fan since his uncle gave him a copy of McLaren's 'Madam Butterfly' in 1989. He was too young to go through the punk era so was approaching it from a different angle. Christakis's theory was that the problem lies in the fact that both McLaren and Lydon were born under the star sign of Aquarius. We live in the age of Aquarius; an age of rebels and rebellion, idealists, modernisation and freedom. On the downside, some astrologers believed that it was a time of non-conformity, irresolution, mental diseases and nervous disorders.

Chris develops the idea. 'This is a time for breaking down boundaries. I believe the rules one generation breaks down cause the next generation to behave the way they do. However, where the Aquarius is concerned, we have the difficult task of breaking two generations of rules down in one lifetime. We have to constantly stay ahead of the game in order to put our point across.

'Change must occur but in order for it to make an impact it has to move two steps ahead. That was basically Malcolm McLaren's ideology for the Sex Pistols. By creating such havoc, but with a foundation, this "movement" was allowed to flourish in many ways. Politically, sexually, fashion-wise, musically.

'With both McLaren and Lydon being Aquarius there was a double-edged sword with both personalities wanting and needing to take centre stage. However, with McLaren being the intelligent man he was, taking centre stage meant taking a back seat. He had no problem with Lydon and later Vicious being at the front of the movement, as he could behave how he wanted, watch and learn and carry on creating and imagining the Pistols in and out of each situation.'

The point of the Sex Pistols was always morals. The Pistols had a delicate balance of good and bad. With

McLaren and the Pistols, a rare combination of good and bad was combined in the best possible way to challenge society's morals, with your laddish role model at the forefront voicing lyrics applicable to a working-class culture, but instructed and created by a far more 'fey' middle class. Thus was created an incredible amalgam of male values and aspirations, fighting together, yet underneath there was this conflict between the two men.

Interesting that in 2010 we have a hung parliament with men realising that to make this country work we must work together. A lyric spoken by the World's Famous Supreme Team on *Duck Rock*, I may hasten to add.

It is interesting to note that, shortly after the punk revolution, Thatcher was voted into power, forcing Britain into an uncreative, scientific, insipid state of mind, the results of which are still being felt today.

McLaren's heritage is his vision, as it showed what could happen when people worked together.

McLaren wrote an article in the *Evening Standard* about Lydon when John was playing out his cartoon punk act on *I'm A Celebrity*... 'He was always an outsider in the Sex Pistols. What you have to remember is that Johnny came from a nice Irish Catholic family in Finsbury Park, North London, and he really did not want to know anyone. He was a good boy trying to be a bad boy and the band knew that.

'People have no idea but, at the time, Rotten – this well-behaved boy – hated the idea of stepping on stage as a Sex Pistol. He hated the name and a lot of the time he hated me.'

McLaren was also approached to do the show and flew for 34 hours to the Australian rain forest. At the last moment he pulled out fearing that he would not be paid the agreed fee of almost £500,000. He told the *Daily Mail*, 'The whole show is a circus. Viewers need to wake up to the fact that the celebs are just a motley crew in ITV's horror movie and basically I am no longer interested in the script.'

McLaren was becoming a little weary that the adjectives most applied him to were 'crazy', 'lunatic', 'non-conformist' and 'unreliable'. He was now in his sixties and his last few stunts were made particularly poignant by the knowledge that he did not have long to live.

His relationship with his mother was never resolved. Once, in the early '80s, while travelling to Liverpool Street station on the London tube, Malcolm looked up and saw his mother who had boarded the train at Stratford, sitting opposite. For the length of the journey, they never exchanged a word. They were to meet up just once more at the end of the decade. His girlfriend at the time, Lauren Hutton, persuaded him to try to reconcile with her. They met one Christmas at his brother's house in St Albans but it went rather badly. McLaren was so nervous at the prospect of meeting his mother he hid in the bathroom when she arrived. The meeting dissolved when she became upset at the conversation turning to the subject of Peter McLaren. As Malcolm left, his mother stated that McLaren was 'the spitting image of his grandmother, the most hideous woman on the planet'.

McLaren never saw his mother again: a few weeks later she died from a heart attack.

Another of his major relationships, with Vivienne Westwood, had crashed and burned years ago. They never married and the business was dissolved. Vivienne went on to embrace the haute couture mainstream and accepted an OBE, later upgraded to DBE. McLaren once admitted that 'secretly she wanted to dress the Queen'. In a Questions & Answers slot for the *Independent*, he extended the point. 'Vivienne gets lost in the theatrical design of clothes. Clothes and ideas that would be better used in a lesson on the history of dress. Vivienne is a fine designer but her work in the commercial field seemed to make more sense back in the '80s.

'We need survival kits. Romantic clothes that are organic and can claim to be part of the generation that cares.'

McLaren said this at the start of the 21st century and once again was chillingly accurate with his reference to 'survival kits' .With the world engulfed in the worst financial crisis since the 1930s, survival was taking precedence over romance.

Freelance writer and DJ Julian Rigby told an amusing story of a meeting one night with McLaren in a London drinking club. It was the time McLaren was working with The Wild Strawberries, three attractive young Chinese girls. McLaren was also experimenting with 'chip music', created by hacking into old video game sound cartridges. He loved it and was connecting it up with punk rock because it was so DIY. Rigby had a computer background and was intrigued that he could make music out of technology. They spent a very amusing time sipping Chablis grand cru and hatching schemes, and at the end of it McLaren handed Rigby his card, a highly embossed, important-looking object. The next morning, Rigby fished the card out of his jacket and found that it just said 'Malcolm McLaren' on it with no telephone, mobile or email on it. He wondered how many of them were scattered across the globe.

McLaren died of mesothelioma – a rare form of cancer that is almost certainly caused by previous exposure to asbestos. Malignant cells develop in the mesothelium, a protective lining that covers most of the body's internal organs. Its most common site is the outer lining of the lungs and chest cavity. McLaren had been diagnosed with the cancer for some time but kept it quiet and maintained a low profile, supported by Young

Kim. In October 2009, it came back, and McLaren saw cancer specialists in London, Paris and New York. The same disease killed the actor Steve McQueen, and, like McQueen, McLaren had sought alternative methods to fight the disease in the last few months of his life. This involved looking at his diet and a treatment involving mistletoe, but nothing could save him.

It was hinted that McLaren could have inhaled asbestos particles or been exposed to asbestos dust in, of all places, 430 King's Road, when the shop was being refurbished, or possibly when he tore a huge hole in the ceiling and put up pictures of the RAF bombing of the German city of Dresden.

McLaren died with a joke on his lips, as he had lived. His stepson Ben visited him on his deathbed wearing a Westwood-designed T-shirt bearing the slogan 'Free Leonard Peltier'. Peltier had been jailed in 1977 for the murder of two FBI agents. Supporters of Peltier claimed that his conviction was one of the greatest miscarriages of justice in the history of the American legal system. He is due for release in 2040.

On the last day of his life, McLaren was slipping in and out of consciousness. At one point he awoke, saw Ben in the corner and motioned for him to come close.

'Free Leonard Peltier,' he muttered. Though some might have heard 'Who Killed Bambi?'